ABANDONED?

AUSTRALIANS AT SANDAKAN 1945

DON WALL

Foreword

I appreciate very much the honour of the author's invitation to me to write a foreword to his study of the circumstances which had bearing upon the atrocity that the Japanese Army perpetrated on the 2500 odd Australian and British prisoners of war at Sandakan in 1944/45.

It must be realised that until March 1944 when Captain Steele was evacuated by submarine from Mindanao to Australia, nothing concrete was known to the Allies about what happened to British, Australian or Indian prisoners of war after the fall of Singapore.

When the S.R.D. clandestine party was inserted into North Borneo in October 1943 neither that party nor their directing organisation, the Allied Intelligence Bureau (A.I.B.) had any knowledge of the large concentration of POW's only 100 miles away at Sandakan.

The mission of that party was to establish observation posts overlooking the Sibutu channel to report the movement of Japanese shipping, particularly the oil carriers from Balikpapan and Tarakan. A secondary role was to contact agents in the coastal strip between Sandakan and Tarakan with the object of setting up an intelligence network.

Thus the consideration of the possible reaction of the Japanese, if that party's presence, so close to the POW camp became known to them, was not a factor considered in the planning.

As soon as the existence of the POW camp became known in Australia, Services Reconnaissance Department (S.R.D.), the cover name for Special Operations Australia (S.O.A.) made an appreciation of the situation and submitted an outline plan to G.H.Q. through A.I.B. for a rescue operation – this plan was code named 'Kingfisher'.

This would have been approximately July 1944, at which stage

Allied forces had reached Hollandia and fighting in the Aitape/Wewak area was still in progress, nearly 1000 miles east of Morotai.

In the broader sphere one must examine and appreciate broad strategic decisions which had already been taken at Joint Chiefs of Staff and theatre level. It had been agreed at that level that the object to be achieved was the defeat of Japan in its homeland as that would end the war in the Pacific quickly and obviate the necessity of attacking and recapturing all of Japan's far flung conquests in Asia one by one.

Further MacArthur's own outline forecast of operations which had been submitted to and received the nod from the Joint Chiefs of Staff in Washington included the capture of Morotai and (Nimitz's) capture of Palau in September 1944. This was to be followed by the invasion of the Philippines in October 1944 (Mindanao, changed to Leyte) and Dec 1944 (put back to Jan 1945) Luzon.

Only one who has experienced in operational and logistic planning at the highest level can appreciate the enormous task of planning the detailed requirements of troops, warships, aircraft carriers, ammunition, equipment, stores, medical supplies, rations, fuel, shipping and transport aircraft etc, against a terribly tight deadline such as was involved in this major operation.

It was into this atmosphere that the outline plan of 'Kingfisher' to rescue the POW's at Sandakan was injected and considered by the joint service planners under MacArthur. The first and obvious decision was that it could not be considered until after Morotai was captured and land based air support came within range of Sandakan.

The operation would otherwise require carrier borne air support with the co-committment of naval escort and logistic shipping support. This was all fully committed to the capture of Morotai and Palau and subsequent operations against the Philippines.

Even after the capture of Morotai the logistic build up and troop movement on and into that island as a forward base for the invasion of the Philippines would have allowed little scope for an extra operation such as 'Kingfisher' which would have required considerable naval, air and logistic support, almost certainly including a 600 bed hospital ship.

War is essentially cruel and brutal and in the execution of the principal object no activity which does not contribute to the achievement of that object (in this case the earliest possible defeat of Japan in its homeland) can be entertained.

The amended plan for 'Kingfisher' proposed for November 1944 involved a combined naval and airborne operation, the operational and logistic requirements of which would have seriously detracted from the main operations in the Philippines and accordingly could not be approved.

The Allied bombing of Sandakan in October 1944 and onwards was aimed at putting that airfield out of action to prevent Japanese air reinforcement during the Leyte landings and the subsequent operations in the Sulu archipelago and Luzon.

This study by Don Wall, I consider, has been well worthwhile as it has put into a coherent perspective a lot of happenings and activities most people had thought to be unrelated.

A great deal of research by the author has gone into this work which also includes quite a bit of first hand personal recollection of some of the participants in the events described, which I think, helps its 'readability'.

There is some well reasoned conjecture included regarding the possible plans prepared by the POWs themselves if a rescue operation were made which, I think may help the reader feel something of the inside of a POW camp.

Don Wall's story should help strongly to answer the unwarranted and misguided suggestion that the Australian and British prisoners at Sandakan were callously abandoned by the American High Command.

I am glad to have been able to read this book which I consider will interest those who want to know what went on behind the scenes, but more tragically, it will interest the relatives of those who suffered so cruelly at the hands of the Japanese.

C.H. Finlay
Major General (Ret.)
June 1990

By the same Author:
Singapore and Beyond
Sandakan – The Last March

Published by D. Wall
98 Darley Street West, Mona Vale,
NSW 2103 Australia.

Printed by Griffin Press, Adelaide, S.A. 5000
Typesetting by Budget Type & Art, Mona Vale.

ISBN 0 7316 9169 5

Contents

Chapter 1   THE SANDAKAN TRAGEDY

Chapter 2   GUERILLAS IN THE PHILIPPINES

Chapter 3   PYTHON

Chapter 4   PLANS FOR RELIEF OF SANDAKAN PRISONERS
             OF WAR

Chapter 5   MACARTHUR PLANS THE CAPTURE OF BRITISH
             NORTH BORNEO

Chapter 6   OBOE 1 – TARAKAN

Chapter 7   WHY A RESCUE NEVER MATERIALISED

Chapter 8   IT'S THE NOT KNOWING.......

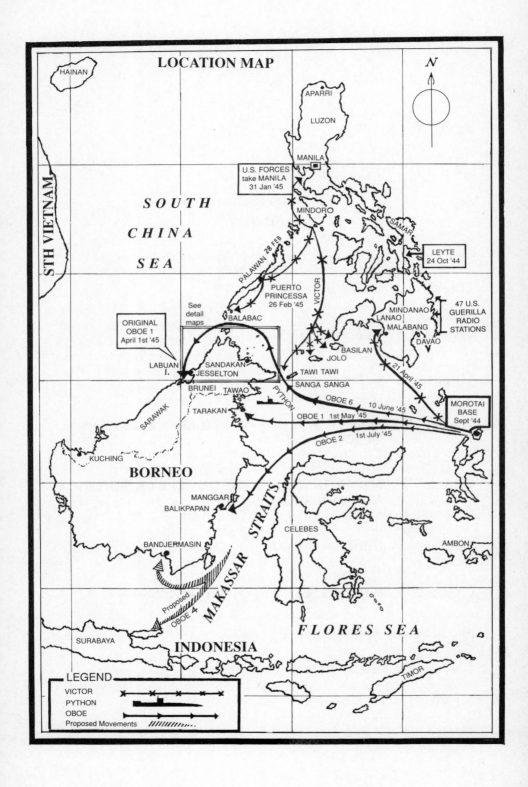

LOCATION MAP

N

HAINAN

STH VIETNAM

SOUTH CHINA SEA

APARRI

LUZON

MANILA

U.S. FORCES take MANILA 31 Jan '45

MINDORO

SAMAR

PALAWAN 28 FEB

PUERTO PRINCESSA 26 Feb '45

VICTOR

LEYTE 24 Oct '44

See detail maps

BALABAC

ORIGINAL OBOE 1 April 1st '45

MINDANAO
LANAO
MALABANG

DAVAO

47 U.S. GUERILLA RADIO STATIONS

LABUAN I.

SANDAKAN JESSELTON

BASILAN
JOLO

21 April '45

BRUNEI   TAWAO

TAWI TAWI

TARAKAN

SANGA SANGA

PYTHON

OBOE 6

10 June '45

MOROTAI BASE Sept '44

SARAWAK

OBOE 1 1st May '45

KUCHING

OBOE 2   1st July '45

BORNEO

MANGGAR

BALIKPAPAN

CELEBES

AMBON

BANDJERMASIN

MAKASSAR STRAITS

Proposed OBOE 4

SURABAYA

INDONESIA

FLORES SEA

TIMOR

LEGEND

VICTOR
PYTHON
OBOE
Proposed Movements

Introduction

"Sandakan – The Last March" published in 1988 honoured and identified 1,800 Australians who died in North Borneo 1942–1945 as prisoners of the Japanese, and also honoured the 711 British who died there.

Of the 1800 Australians 600 were married – they left their wives and children and volunteered to join the Australian Imperial Forces when they believed Australia was in grave danger, becoming prisoners of war after the fall of Singapore. Their widows were informed the briefest details of their deaths as prisoners of war in Borneo, sadly, the children had to wait until they were adults to find out what had happened to their Father, brother or uncle.

The first set-back for the prisoners at Sandakan occurred when the Intelligence group within and outside the camp collapsed in July 1943. Following many arrests of loyal natives, Captain Matthews, Lieuts. Weynton and Wells, with a number of technicians, were taken into the custody of the Kempe Tai. Many disclosures followed. After finding a receiving wireless and a transmitter under construction Matthews was tried at Kuching and condemned; Weynton, Wells and several other men were sentenced to terms of imprisonment – all but eight of the officers were removed to Kuching.

The details of this event are from Japanese translation to portray their reaction to what was to become known as "The Sandakan Incident." This account details the chain of events which contributed in some way to the plight and ultimate fate of the prisoners of war at Sandakan.

Within six months three Commandos of PYTHON party were caught in January and February 1944 within 100 miles of Sandakan; they were taken to Sandakan Gaol where they were brutally tortured by the same Kempe Tai who tortured Matthews and the other party. The Japanese reacted by introducing a starvation program to reduce the POWs to an ineffective force in the event of an Allied invasion. Additional troops were also moved in to guard the airfield the POWs were building.

In 1947, General Blamey, speaking at a Reunion, stated the prisoners could have been rescued if General Headquarters had provided air transport for the rescue operation. This statement did not take into account the complexities of an operation of this magnitude. A plan was drawn up and reached G.H.Q. where it was examined and abandoned as impracticable at the time. In considering any rescue proposal G.H.Q. would have to take into account the overall assessment of possible repercussions throughout the South West Pacific Command where Camps containing many thousands of POWs were located. Sandakan could not be considered in isolation to these.

Major Rex Blow, D.S.O., Mentioned in Despatches, renowned Australian Guerilla Leader who had escaped from Borneo and fought on in Mindanao until April 1945 when he was evacuated to Morotai, where he met General Blamey, after a long yarn asked him, "What about the blokes at Sandakan," and General Blamey replied, "If a rescue can be fitted into forthcoming operations it would be done."

"ABANDONED" details the 'forthcoming operation' and the many changes which took place – events which contributed to the fate of the POWs at Sandakan. It exposes the mis-information the Dutch supplied to G.H.Q. to influence the order and choice of Tarakan as OBOE 1. By this unfortunate change the Japanese were able to successfully tie down the 26 Brigade, which was destined to relieve Sandakan, for several weeks.

During this period the Commander of the S.R.D. party operating north of Sandakan was extracted by Catalina for de-briefing. He stated on May 20, 1945 there were no prisoners of war at Sandakan. On May 27, Allied aircraft attacked the camp where there were still 900 POWs, killing many.

By May 29 the Japanese had panicked – the second march was on its way and those left behind perished. Time had now run out for the prisoners of war; the 26 Brigade was still deeply involved on Tarakan. For those remaining in the jungle on the road to Ranau there was little hope - two escaped from the march and four escaped and were rescued by special forces in the Ranau area.

Captain Yamamoto who was in charge of the first death march to Ranau, when interrogated by War Crimes Officers was asked, "What happened to those prisoners who could not continue on the march?" and he replied, "They were abandoned."

Schedule of Events

December 8, 1941	Japan attacks and declares War on Britain and United States.
February 15, 1942	Singapore falls.
April 1942	American and Filipino forces surrender at Bataan.
May 1942	General Wainwright surrenders at Corregidor.
July 1942	1500 Australian prisoners of War sent to Sandakan, British North Borneo, to construct an airfield.
November 1942	POWs in Sandakan Camp establish Intelligence Group in liaison with local police to assist Allied invasion.
April 1943	750 British POWs arrive from Java and 500 Australian POWs from Singapore arrive in Sandakan and are kept in separate compound.
June 1943	Eight Australians escape from Berhala Island in Sandakan Harbour.
July 1943	Captain Matthews and many POWs and Natives arrested. Intelligence Organisation collapses.
September 1943	All but eight of the Officers removed from Sandakan to Kuching.
October 1943	Australian Commando Party, code-named PYTHON, land within 100 miles of Sandakan POW Camp; establish Observation Station

overlooking Sibutu Channel and radio contact with Australia.

November 1943	Escaped POWs from Sandakan reach Mindanao.
December 1943	The Australians, Blow, Gillon, Steele and McLaren, join Colonel Wendell Fertig's Guerilla organisation – Lt. Wagner killed in action.
January 1944	PYTHON reinforced by Phase 11 and lose Sgt. Brandis.
February 1944	Japanese begin search for PYTHON party; Captain Steele receives order to be evacuated from Mindanao by submarine to Australia; Japanese capture Rudwick and McKenzie.
March 1944	Major Jinkins evacuated by USS NARWHAL; Captain Steele on same submarine; Captain Matthews shot by firing squad.
April 1944	Japanese react to presence of Australians close to POW Camp ordering rice ration to be reduced.
June 1944	Last of PYTHON evacuated by USS HARDER. Sandakan POWs now on starvation ration.
July 1944	Last Japanese ship into Sandakan.
September 1944	Allied Invasion Forces take Morotai 650 miles from Sandakan. Lt. Rudwick, Sgts. Brandis and McKenzie taken from Sandakan to Jesselton for trial.
October 1944	U.S. Forces land on Leyte; bombing commences at Sandakan.
November 1944	Allied planes over Sandakan almost daily.
December 1944	Australian Commandos Rudwick, McKenzie and Brandis sentenced to death. B24s blast Sandakan Christmas Day.
January 1945	General Baba takes command of Japanese 37 Army in Borneo. POWs cease work on airfield; first death march of 470 leave Sandakan for Ranau, escorted by Yamamoto's Unit.

Chapter 1

"I asked the Jap guard if I could go to the toilet – he said okay but insisted I go about a hundred yards away and at the same time remain in sight. I dug a hole and not far away I heard a voice, "Don't look up or look startled," he said. I cautiously looked at the figure who was wearing a beret and camouflaged uniform and carrying a sub-machine gun of a type I had never seen before. I said, "Who are you?", he did not reply. "Are you a Yank?", "No", he said. "Are you an Australian?" but he did not reply. Then he quickly asked me how many POWs in the camp, I told him there used to be about two thousand but some have been moved on and there are a lot dying; he asked how many fit men there were and I said we could get about three to four hundred. "Could they be armed", he asked, "we have some arms but not enough, how often do you come out here?" "Every day", I said. "You find out how many are in the camp and I'll come back tomorrow or the next day – see your Officer but don't tell anyone else" – related Gunner Owen Campbell, one of the six survivors from the 2500 sent to Sandakan.

This meeting took place in April 1945 in the Sibuga River area between the airfield and the river. Campbell reported the meeting to Captain Picone, the Medical Officer, who supplied him with figures and warned him not to talk to anyone in the camp about the meeting. Next day Campbell was again placed in the wood party but the mystery figure was not seen again. He could not for certain determine his nationality.

This was one of the mysteries and haunting stories associated with the dreaded Sandakan prison camp – who was the man in the beret who whispered to Owen Campbell? Whoever he was he vanished from history along with the faint hope of rescue he inspired.

Campbell was real enough. He had been a prisoner of the Japanese since the fall of Singapore in February 1942 and had been in Sandakan since June 1943. There were three groups of Prisoners – the 1500 Australians who arrived in July 1942, 750 British who came from Java via Singapore in April 1943 and 500 Australians who arrived via Berhala Island in June 1943. They were all kept in separate compounds and not permitted to communicate with one another. The prisoners were sent to Sandakan to construct an airfield as part of a strategic network connecting the South West Pacific with the mainland.

When the first party arrived there in July 1942 there were many small groups who decided to escape and head for Australia. At the time the camp perimeter was lightly constructed and guarded; when one group left, a large crowd went down to the fence to see them off and some even sang the "Maori Farewell". It was not long before they were all rounded up and dealt with by the Kempe Tai – 'tried' and sent off to do a stretch at the notorious Outram Road Gaol in

Left: Gnr. Owen Campbell pictured 1941. One of six survivors from Sandakan.
Right: L/Cpl. John Brinkman, NX.32936 Balmain, NSW.
Died 7 March 1945 at Paginatan with rice carrying party.

Shirley Mills

Sandakan POW Camp   *James M. Kendall. 309 Bombardment Group*

Singapore. This turn of events saved many of them from the death marches still to come.

After these early attempts the Camp Commandant, Hoshijima, warned the others that any attempting to escape would be shot. The conditions in the camp were reasonably bearable.

In late 1942 Japanese High Command decided to remove senior Australian officers from the other ranks. Lt. Col. Walsh, the commander of 'B' Force, with several of his senior officers was taken to Kuching where the principal POW and Internees Camp was located under the control of Major Suga. The movement of officers continued until September 1943.

It was in November 1942 a group of technicians, under the control of Capt. Matthews, M.C., in co-operation with the local loyal Constabulary obtained parts to construct a radio. Matthews had been appointed Intelligence Officer after the death of a shadowy figure, Lt. N.K. Sligo, who was given an honorary commission by order of Malaya Command and sent with the Australians. It is understood he was selected for this task as he had considerable knowledge of the Islands in the vicinity of Borneo. His death in late August 1942, is only mentioned in Col. Walsh's Roll.

Matthews appointed his own Signals Officer to assist him organise liaison with the local Constabulary and many other loyal natives. The organisation operated successfully until it collapsed in July 1943 – Matthews, a Signals Officer, had distinguished himself during the fighting in Malaya was awarded the Military Cross, took no action to insulate his identity or his assistants from the native contacts – the whole camp seemed to know where the radio was kept and even the friendly old Japanese Quartermaster, Ichikawa, who understood and spoke English, overheard the prisoners discussing the news and warned them to be more careful.

The Power Station was located outside the Sandakan camp perimeter, and Matthews had been successful in persuading Hoshijima there were competent mechanical technicians in the camp capable of operating the steam driven generator. This crew were permitted to talk to the other civilians working there and acted as couriers to friends in Sandakan and Berhala Island where the civilians were interned up to January 1943, when they were moved to Kuching.

The Kempe Tai employed a number of civilians as spies to watch the natives who made contact with the prisoners. One of these reported Joo Ming, who had assisted Wallace's escape in April 1943. It was not long before he was picked up by the Kempe Tai and from the brutal interrogation names started to flow. The first arrests were made on July 18, 1943, and as the torture continued more names surfaced – Capt. Matthews, Lt. Weynton and Lt. Wells, who worked on the wood party to keep the Power House going. Matthews was soon arrested and while he remained unbreakable, others broke; altogether more than thirty POWs were rounded up and eventually sent off to Kuching for Trial. The Japanese reacted by removing all but eight of the officers to Kuching.

At this time there were no other repercussions; life settled down to hard work for those who marched to the airfield each day – sickness was beginning to mount, mainly amongst the older men. There were many who had served in World War 1 and they must have wondered to themselves: "What the hell am I doing here!"

It was not till early 1944 the rations were reduced, the prisoners were now feeling the effects of these cuts. They were not to know the reason. The only news of the war they were receiving was from the Japanese and from their own optimistic accounts. Names previously unknown to men were now being mentioned – they realised the Allies were now on the move. In June 1943, following the escape of eight 'E' Force officers and men, the Kempe Tai tightened further control over movement of native craft and prohibited kumpits to a range of 10 miles from Sandakan without special passes and identification. A strict control was also placed on boat building, this action restricted the natives in the freedom of trade they previously enjoyed with the Sulu Islands.

By the end of 1943 optimism prevailed among the prisoners despite the number of men suffering from malaria, beri-beri and ulcers. The guards maintained pressure on the airfield construction where a second strip was now well under way. The airfield site was well above water level and was being top-dressed with coral from the adjoining hills. The glare of the sun on the light coloured material affected the already weakened eyes of the prisoners; as a punishment for any 'misdemeanor' the guards would force the prisoners to stand facing the sun with their arms outstretched, eyes open. There was only one advantage in working on the airfield, the Japanese provided a reasonably good midday meal; this 'bonus' often encouraged hospital patients to ask to be placed on working parties in order to get the extra food. They believed by starving the sick it would force them to work. There were a number of occasions when the guards disregarded the doctor's decision and went into the huts and hounded the sick to the airfield.

The first serious cut in the rice ration occurred about April 1944 – no reason was given. Appeals were made by Capt. Cook, the Camp

Administrator, for more rice, Hoshijima promised the rice would be substituted with tapioca and other root crops and on his own initiative, now increased the size of the vegetable garden.

By June 1944 the rice ration was now reduced to 6ozs. per day from the original 17ozs., sickness increased rapidly. Appeals were made and the usual answer given: "We'll look into it." Hoshijima appealed to Colonel Suga, the Commander of all POW Camps, for more food, each time Suga visited the Camp he would tell the POWs "to look after your healths" and following his return to Kuching the rations seemed to become worse.

In September 1944 after Allied reconnaissance planes had flown over the camp Hoshijima erected a large POW sign just outside the Compound and moved from his own house, (formerly Agnes Keith's home which overlooked Sandakan Harbour,) into Wong's bungalow just outside the No. 1 Camp. The survivors claimed he did this for his own protection; the basement of the house was also used by the Japanese to store almost a thousand bags of rice.

On September 15, 1944, Allied Forces occupied Morotai, just 650 miles away, the guards told the prisoners : "Soon – Americans 'boom' 'boom' Sandakan!" Their prediction was forthcoming; the first bombs fell on October 14 when the airfield was raided, putting the strip out of action and destroying most aircraft – from that day on Lightnings would appear overhead daily, discipline became severe and deaths increased. The POWs were now working at night filling in the craters the planes made during the day. By January, the Japanese gave up all hope of repairing the airfield, and the POWs were now employed growing food to survive.

General Baba, Commander, Japanese Force in Borneo, received orders to concentrate eight of his ten Battalions in the Brunei Bay area and order the Yamamoto Unit to take 500 POWs with him. Hoshijima was unable to supply the 500 fit men and rostered 470 – made up of nine parties escorted by what Baba described as one of his best Units. He was anxious to hasten the march to have his troops in position.

The POWs were told they were being transferred to an area where food was more plentiful. Dan Galton was heard to say: "That's what they told us before we came to Borneo!"

Orang Tuan Kulang of the Muanad area – he was later to become No 1 Agent for the Australian Commandos – assisted in cutting the rentis for the Japanese from the 42 miles in the Muanad area and further west. He had no idea the prisoners of war would be using it and as the Japanese insisted the track avoid all habitation and

Left: Gnr. Archibald John McGlinn, NX.6627, Denistone, NSW. Died Ranau 9 July 1945 E. McGrath
Right: Sig. Theodore R.B. McKay (Served as D.S. McKenzie, QX. 15656) Point Piper, NSW. Escaped with Sig. Harvey, was lured into kampong for food and shot by Kempe Tai, Sandakan 11 May 1943
Sybil Ash

Left: S/Sgt. Robert George Brown, NX.39190. Died 11 July 1945. His identity disc and paybook were found at Ranau. Jill Blayden
Right: Pte. Leslie McGill, NX.54907. Waterloo, NSW. Died Sandakan 11 April 1945. Colleen McGill.

believing they would be the only users of it he cut the rentis over the most difficult terrain.

O.T. Kulang was conducting his own war against the Japanese up to the time he joined the Australian Commandos as an agent. He claims to have killed 96 Japanese – about half by shooting and the rest he killed with his parang – in many instances cutting their heads off – and some he killed with the poison dart.

It was now the wet season and the prisoners marched in mud up to their knees in the low lying areas for the first few days and, despite the hardships, they maintained good morale, believing the Japanese track conditions would improve further on. Kulang observed the prisoners in camp a few days out – he reported seeing some of them shaving, which he found strange, and one night by a camp fire he heard them singing. The singing didn't last long, the camp guards soon put a stop to it. Despite this there were signs of confidence among the POWs. Kulang said the men on the first march were fairly fit and had serviceable clothes and boots, however he did observe many had beri-beri and had swollen feet and could not wear boots. At this time Kulang witnessed the shooting of Pte Haye, which was the first sign that those unable to continue would be callously shot.

Each prisoner had a camp number on a piece of wood attached to his hat or shirt or tied on to his loin cloth – it was this number the Japanese would record when the prisoner died or was shot. These were later translated on to the official record held at the Kuching Compound.

The senior POW in this party was Captain Rod Jeffrey, Medical Officer – without supplies; the party leaders were all senior NCOs. They were under the command of a Japanese officer who had no previous experience in dealing with Allied prisoners of war; behind them were small detachments of Kempe Tai like vultures picking off those who attempted to escape into the jungle. Much of the rentis was a tunnel below the jungle canopy with stubble of undergrowth protruding like large spikes through the mud; it took a heavy toll on the prisoners' feet, the prisoners were too exhausted to talk. The earlier parties had picked any edible fern tops within reach, but despite their exhaustion they shared their last energies helping their mates.

The first habitation encountered was in the Croker Ranges at Paginatan where they were permitted to trade gear they were unable to carry further, for food. Having completed the transaction the Japanese would then confiscate some for themselves. At night the men would huddle under a blanket or ground sheet as it became colder. In the morning those unable to continue would ask their mates to get a message home – if they made it. As the march commenced the sound of gun fire could be heard to the rear and each man wondered when his turn would come.

Of the 470 men who set out from Sandakan about half were to remain at Paginatan to carry rice to Ranau. After a few months only about thirty reached Ranau. In the meantime other parties had reached there earlier; here they came under the command of Captain Nagai who was Hoshijima's Adjutant until he had left Sandakan earlier to command a party of 300 English prisoners at Labuan. After half of those died he was sent to supervise the rice-carrying parties. Keith Botterill remembers the dapper officer who spoke fluent English, wore a white silk shirt and lived in a small hut. Nagai daily recorded the deaths to relay to Kuching.

Back in Sandakan the rice was no longer available to the prisoners, They were to live on produce from the gardens comprising tapioca, sweet potato and kangkong, the ration being determined by Higher Authority. The Camp was now a hospital with everyone suffering from various disabilities and the death rate was escalating daily. During 1944 about 100 died – in January 1945 – 91, in February 1945 – 263, in March 1945 – 310, in April 1945 – 266 and in May 1945 – 202. It was during May the Camp Commandant was replaced by Captain Takakuwa who had been involved in planning the defence of Sandakan and now was ready to execute it.

On May 17, after taking over, he was forewarned to prepare to move all prisoners to Ranau. During this period Allied aircraft were flying over daily – they were now aware the POW sign had been removed. Prisoners working on the garden and wood parties were now being attacked. On May 27 a sustained attack was carried out by U.S. and Australian aircraft supported by U.S. torpedo boats from Tawi Tawi, killing many POWs. The Japanese believed an invasion was imminent and set about planning an evacuation.

On May 29 Takakuwa gave orders to destroy the huts and everything else the prisoners could not carry, including some medical supplies. He estimated he had about 400 stretcher cases and 200 who could not walk and decided to leave 288 behind. He assembled 536 and commenced the second death march. The prisoners prayed that the rumours floating around the camp that they were going to be handed over to the Allies were true. Their hopes disappeared when they left the camp and headed west – some dashed for freedom only to be shot down.

Capt. Watanabe kept the casualty record – with his band of killers they disposed of all those unable to continue. Kulang, now an agent for the Australian commandos, reported to his superiors the events taking place. Only two prisoners were able to escape on the march, Richard Braithwaite and Owen Campbell. On June 26 when 183 survivors reached Ranau expecting to meet their mates from the first march, they found six men alive. The rice-carrying had taken its toll. Early July a party of four, Moxham, Botterill, Anderson and Short, escaped. Anderson died in the jungle, the others were befriended by Bariga and later rescued by Australian Special Forces.

On July 28, W.O. Sticpewich was warned by his friend, Takahara, a Formosan, that the remaining prisoners were going to be killed. He had seen Takakuwa's orders. That night Sticpewich and Reither escaped. They remained within the camp area and observed the search parties searching for them. When the activities died down they moved away from the area. Reither died and Sticpewich was later rescued by Special Forces.

On August 1 Takakuwa gave orders for the last of the prisoners to be massacred. There were only six survivors from Sandakan – all those remaining back at the camp died or were eliminated.

Allied Intelligence Bureau was well informed of the location, identity and number of prisoners in the camp since 1943. In addition they would have been aware of information from the code-breakers on messages sent to Japanese Headquarters in Borneo on policy matters affecting the prisoners.

Special Forces were sent into Borneo in March 1945 to report on the prisoners there. Colonel Suarez, the guerrilla leader on Tawi Tawi, reported on all information coming out of Sandakan to General Headquarters, who were aware of the potential of the airfield being built at Sandakan.

The following Chapters tell of the events which contributed to the fate of 2,500 Australian and British prisoners of war who died there.

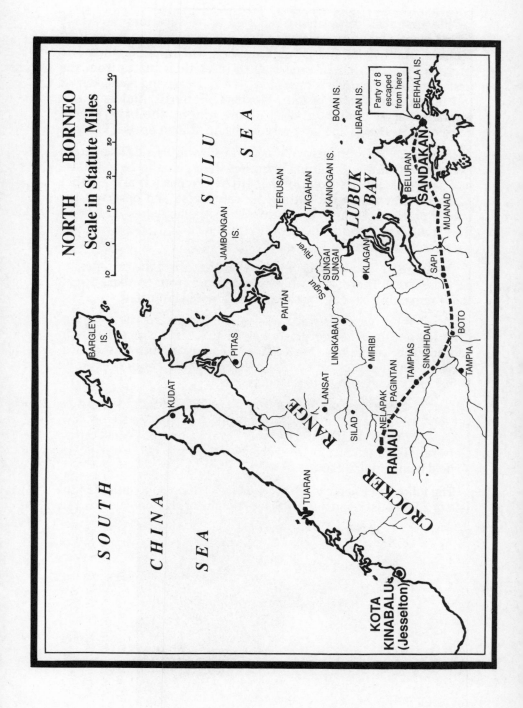

NORTH BORNEO
Scale in Statute Miles

SOUTH
CHINA
SEA

SULU
SEA

Party of 8
escaped
from here

BERHALA IS.

BOAN IS.

LIBARAN IS.

KANIOGAN IS.

TAGAHAN

TERUSAN

JAMBONGAN
IS.

BARGLEY
IS.

PITAS

PAITAN

KUDAT

Sugut River

SUNGAI
SUNGAI

KLAGAN

LUBUK
BAY

BELURAN

SANDAKAN

MUANAD

SAPI

LINGKABAU

MIRIBI

LANSAT

BOTO

SILAD

SINGIHDAI

TAMPIAS

TAMPIA

NELAPAK

PAGINTAN

RANAU

CROCKER RANGE

TUARAN

KOTA
KINABALU
(Jesselton)

From Left: Commander Charles Parsons, General Douglas MacArthur and Captain Charles Smith at G.H.Q. Brisbane 1943. Commander Parsons, following the Japanese Occupation of Manila, claimed Diplomatic status and was repatriated. With Capt. Charles Smith he returned to the Philippines in USS TAMBOR in February 1943 to advise General MacArthur on the recognition of Guerilla leaders and establish a radio network with Australia.

Patrick C. Parsons. Manila

Chapter 2

In March 1942 the Americans were still holding out on Bataan and causing the Japanese heavy casualties and embarrassment; however, the Japanese changed their tactics realising shortage of food and illness would now take their toll of the Americans and Filipinos. Washington assessed their priorities – there was nothing they could do to assist MacArthur in the Philippines – the fight would have to be carried on from Australia. MacArthur was ordered out, however, he left with the message, "I shall return!" General Wainwright was left to command – there were 70,000 men.

On 17 March General Douglas MacArthur arrived in Australia, and the next day a statement announcing his appointment (by agreement between the Australian, United Kingdom and United States Governments) as Supreme Commander of the Allied Forces in the South-West Pacific was released by the Australian Prime Minister, Mr. Curtin.

On 3rd April, with the concurrence of the Governments of the United Kingdom, Australia, New Zealand and the Netherlands, a Pacific Area and a South-West Pacific Area were defined by the American Joint Chiefs of Staff at Washington.

MacArthur was told that the Combined Chiefs of Staff would exercise general jurisdiction over the grand strategic policy and over such related factors as were necessary for the proper implementation including the allocation of forces and war material; and that the United States Joint Chiefs of Staff would exercise jurisdiction over all matters pertaining to operational strategy.

Immediate results of the operational-area division of the Pacific, and of the directives to the area commanders were the allocation of all combat sections of the Australian defence services to the South-

West Pacific Area, and the notifications to their commanders that, from midnight on Saturday 18th April, 1942, all orders and instructions issued by General MacArthur in conformity with his directive would be considered by them as emanating from the Australian Government.

Now within the new South West Pacific Command the story of North Borneo cannot be treated in isolation to the Philippines. The events unfolding there with regard to Prisoners of War would influence the Joint Chiefs of Staff and General MacArthur in formulating a policy in dealing with their relief.

By April 9 Major General King, the Commander of the beleaguered America Filipino Forces, was forced to recognise the men under his command were no longer a fighting force and would soon be annihilated. Wainwright had ordered King to fight to the death – he saw no point in continuing to sacrifice the men under him, under a flag of truce he drove to Honma's Headquarters where he requested U.S. trucks be allowed to transport the troops to detention camps. He was told surrender must be unconditional. "Will they be treated well?" he asked. "We are not barbarians", said the Japanese, and with that reply Maj.Gen. King handed over his pistol – as a token of surrender.

The "Battling Bastards" were now herded together and set out on what was to become one of the major atrocities of the Pacific War – a 60 mile march to San Fernando – these men, with empty stomachs and illness, dropped out by the hundreds and what was occurring had all the marks of Colonel Tsuji upon it. He was known to have favoured the elimination of prisoners of war and was now conveying orders to individual commanders implying that the Emperor believed it was a good opportunity to get rid of the prisoners, furthermore, it could influence General Wainwright, who was still holding out on Corregidor, to surrender.

Of the 70,000 Filipinos and Americans who surrendered at Bataan 54,000 arrived at Camp O'Donnell – of the 12,000 Americans about 3000 died on the march. The Japanese left a trail of deliberate massacre. No records have emerged which show that Emperor Hirohito ever disciplined any of his Ministers for the march, which would suggest Tsuji was carrying out his wishes.

While the Americans were recovering from the horrendous events in the Philippines the British and Australian POWs in Singapore were suffering from recurrence of malaria and wounds suffered during the fighting; while the working parties had nothing to complain about except scrotal dermatitis. If the hostilities had ended at the end of 1942 in Singapore there would not have been so much hatred towards the Japanese, however, what the Japanese did in Bataan was still to happen to the British and Australians elsewhere. Details of those events were still not known to the outside world.

The Japanese were principally concerned in building up a strong air defensive system in South East Asia – all existing fields were under repair and a substantial number of new fields were on the planning boards. In the Philippines U.S. prisoners were now being sent to Palawan to construct new fields – there the Japanese possessed only captured equipment for construction work; many of these machines were sabotaged thus causing them to use more labour which required large numbers of Asians using small hand-held cane baskets to carry rock and fill – as they had done for hundreds of years – to meet the production requirements for the construction of modern airfields.

Early May 1942 General Wainwright, the American Commander in Chief in the Philippines, was still holding out on the fortress of Corregidor. The Japanese established a foothold on the island while their aircraft were able to pinpoint the huge guns with accurate bombing – it was just a matter of time before the fortress would be overrun. Wainwright decided to seek a truce with General Honma, the Commander of the Japanese Forces, and surrender Corregidor in order to save further loss of life. This was not acceptable to Honma who insisted as Commander in Chief he surrender all U.S. and Filipino Forces in the whole of the Commonwealth. This included General Sharp, whose forces were comparatively intact in Mindanao. MacArthur, now in Australia, informed General Sharp to disregard Wainwright's order. General Honma warned Wainwright that if he did not comply with his order those prisoners of war already held could suffer. Sharp was fully aware of these consequences if he did not also comply with Honma's order, and on 7 May 1942 resistance ceased in the Philippines. Sharp previously gave these officers and men the chance to remain free and fight on if they chose to do so.

There were some thousands of Americans in Japanese captivity – the Japanese were now demonstrating their brutality on those held. In Mindanao there were many Americans who chose to remain free; among these was Wendell Fertig, a Mining Engineer from Colorado, who was operating there at the outbreak of hostilities when he was enlisted in the Army Airforce to supervise the construction of air fields, also Charles Hedges, an engineer associated with the timber industry in the Province of Lanao in Central Mindanao. Hedges had a particularly good knowledge of the island and was on good terms with the Moro, the Muslims who had a long history of fighting the Christians since the 15th Century. These two officers were to play an important role in the formation of the Mindanao Guerillas.

The Japanese rounded up all the American personnel together with the thousands of Filipino soldiers and concentrated them in what was known as the Penal Colony, north of Davao. In pre-war times there were in the order of 18,000 Japanese residents located there – the largest concentration of Japanese outside the homeland of Japan – the locality seemed a safe place for them to be held. The Japanese soon again demonstrated their harsh treatment of the POWs and between May – September 1942, 20,000 Filipinos – and several thousand Americans died at this camp – their treatment was consistent with that demonstrated in other camps in Asia, however the Japanese thought the camp, being surrounded by thick jungle, was impenetrable and safe.

In the meantime at Manila the British and American civilians were systematically rounded up. The Japanese businessmen who were established there pre-war were also spies for the various Armed services and kept records of every foreigner – executives for organisations such as the large Merchant houses emerged as the new leaders of the Philippines. They interned the civilians in the Santo Tomas University – one of those who was not in a hurry to be

Major Rex Blow, D.S.O., Mentioned in Despatches

picked up was local stevedoring businessman Charles Parsons who was principally involved in the shipment of manganese and other minerals. When the Japs called on him and found he was displaying the Panamanian flag, he remembered some time ago he had been appointed their Consul. What the Japs didn't know was that he was also a member of the U.S. Navy Intelligence. Parsons sat tight, demanding he be treated with courtesy and customs of the foreign Diplomatic Corps. The Japanese who were delegated to get the economy underway were anxious to use Parsons' services, offering him various proposals to assist in moving the vast amounts of ore from the Islands for shipment to Japan. Parsons played his cards close to his chest and was repatriated with all other foreign nationals by a Swedish ship, eventually arriving in New York. He quickly reported to the U.S. Navy on all events up to the time of his departure from Manila. His detailed report reached General MacArthur who then made arrangements for Parsons to be posted to South West Pacific Command at Brisbane.

Back on Mindanao the Japanese began occupying and looting everything worthwhile from the storehouses for shipment to Japan and, in the course of these acquisitions, plundered towns and villages, committing rape and murder and generally creating the climate for the formation of resistance guerilla bands.

Pre-war, the Japanese Fifth Column was particularly active and now these local contacts were appointed to civilian administration posts, including the Bureau of the Constabulary and other Government bodies. These collaborators were to be the first victims to succumb to the local guerillas. The first to emerge in central Mindanao was William Tait – American-Negro-Filipino – formerly Chief of Police of one of the provincial towns under the Japanese. It was in September 1942 he decided to revolt. He had made prior arrangements with Luis Morgan, American Mestizo, Police Officer. They crossed Penguil Bay in a sail boat with 34 poorly armed men from Baroy and Kolumbungan areas. Their mission was to surprise Japanese sponsored officers in other Municipalities and take their arms and ammunition ready for distribution to the Japanese. They met no opposition and the mission was successful. Tait arrested officials and ordered them gaoled. Together with Morgan he moved from village to village recruiting new members and appointing new officials.

At this time the movement grew beyond the ability of Morgan and Tait to manage – they were now fighting old enemies, the Moro; the situation was getting out of hand. Morgan had known Hedges in the lumber business and he knew he was friendly and in touch with Wendell Fertig; he decided to approach him to suggest Lt.Col. Fertig take command of the Guerilla Movement.

Fertig was convinced it was a matter of time before he was approached to unify all the guerillas under one command. The Movement was born October 1942.

Fertig was now in touch with various groups hiding out in the rain forest – one group comprised Charles Smith, John Hamner and Albert Y. Smith; they came out of the jungle to seek Fertig's assistance in providing a sail boat for them to escape to Australia – quite a wild idea. Fertig had asked Smith if he knew anything about navigation – he replied Australia was big enough, they would find it. Fertig wished them well.

Early January 1943 a specialist group was now endeavouring to contact the outside world with a crudely constructed transmitter, throughout the night on shifts they began calling up any one prepared to listen – this procedure went on for some weeks when they were picked up by a monitoring station in Washington. The call-sign was one which formerly belonged to an Air Corps station at Del Monte and Washington suspected the call-sign to be from the Japanese. Another operator at Fertig's H.Q. commenced attempts to make contact; it was not till February contact was made with MacArthur's H.Q. through KAZ which was the R.A.A.F. station at Darwin. The call-sign from Fertig to Australia was recognised by Charles Smith who had now arrived in Australia; when he left Fertig he said – "if you make it call-sign would be Smith Fertig Mindanao." Official contact was made on 23 February 1943 when MacArthur sent the first message designating Mindanao as the 10 Military District. Many other units on other islands were now designated and leaders confirmed. However Mindanao remained the stronghold of the organisation.

In Australia, Charles Parsons arrived in Brisbane and was warmly greeted by MacArthur who, after a long chat, told Parsons plans for supporting and reinforcing the Guerillas in the Philippines. The plans outlined were to establish a radio base in the Philippines; Major Villamor, with a party left Australia on the USS GUDGEON and after aborting a landing at Pagadian Bay, southern Mindanao, landed on Negros and established contact with Australia.

MacArthur was now aware there were other guerila leaders jockeying for command and decided to send Lt.Commander Charles Parsons and Charles Smith (now Lt.Col.) to establish what was now known as SPRYON network of radio stations throughout the military districts and to report on the suitability of the various officers chasing command. At this time Morgan had convinced Fertig he should promote himself to Brigadier General in order to

Major Ray Steele, D.S.O.

impress the Filipinos of the importance MacArthur placed on his command.

Parsons left Fremantle in March on the USS TAMBOR and arrived off Pagadian in March with 5 new radio sets and vital supplies.

Fertig was pleased to meet Parsons, who quickly quizzed him as to his mission – they had known one another in better days in Manila. Parsons told him his intelligence gathering had absolute first priority – the guerillas were not to go looking for traitors, their function was to protect the radio network. Parsons was to spend the next 6 months travelling throughout the Philippines without detection.

One of the important missions was for Charles Smith's party to establish a radio watcher station as close as possible to Davao, the Japanese stronghold.

By May 1943 further stations came into commission and G.H.Q. commenced sending in additional radio technicians to support the network. It was early May that Captain Hamner returned. His special mission was to report to Fertig and set up three stations in the

Sulu, with the principal station at Tawi Tawi to report on the shipping through the Sibutu Channel. It was this station which would play the principal role in reporting intelligence from Lt. Col. Suarez on Borneo and the escaped Australian POWs.

The Japanese were now aware of the increased radio traffic operating in the islands and decided to mount an offensive against the unoccupied towns around the coast. Rewards were offered for heads of the guerillas – the Filipinos remained loyal; while MacArthur's submarines carried evidence of increased aid it was not till later that he was able to secure the services of the super submarines to carry large tonnages to the guerillas.

In April 1943 ten American officers escaped from the Penal Colony Camp in the Province of Davao, the largest concentration of prisoners in the Philippines. They had no idea of the developments which had taken place in the Guerilla Organisation after the fall of Bataan and Corregidor. With the guidance of two Filipinos and an oil company road map they figured they would head north away from their jungle gaol and somehow get hold of a sailing boat and head for Australia. The party comprised Commander Melvyn McCoy,

Lt. Charles Wagner, D.C.M., Mentioned in Despatches. Killed Illigan, 21 December 1943.   *John McGrory*

21

Lt.Col. Dyess from the Army Airforce, Major Mellnik of the U.S. Army and several other officers of specialist qualifications. On their map was an indication there was a lumber railway which operated to the north and ran down to Davao. As mentioned, Davao, the capital of the Province, was the most populated Japanese area outside the Japanese homeland and heading south would have meant a collision course with the Japanese.

For some months the officers used their position to acquire the vital supplies for such a risky venture. They all felt after the many deaths of the POWs unless someone got out and told the free world what had happened at the Bataan Death March and the high death toll in the POW Camps there would be no survivors; one of the party, – Sam Grashio, was appointed Chaplain by the party and each night he led them in prayer – they seemed to have needed it, as the shock of finding themselves in a hostile environment could have bewildered them until they became accustomed to the jungle and all the sounds.

They were not to know that a very professional Filipino officer, Captain Laureto, had established a guerilla band in Davao and placed scouts on the perimeter of the POW Camp. The Japs were constantly sending out patrols to keep the natives and the guerillas under control and now with a number of senior officers on the loose a large patrol was despatched to hunt them down.

On the second day they located the rail-road running to the north east; fortunately the two Filipino inmates of the colony escaped with them and were used as forward scouts. They found evidence that a Jap patrol had been in the area – the Japs always left their tell-tale marks of untidiness. These signs put the men on edge walking through strange jungle expecting confrontation at any time. After several days out contact was made with one of the guerillas who suspiciously gave the party a thorough going over – suspecting the Japs had sent decoys ahead to trap the escapees. However, after checking their credentials they were passed on to the next command, eventually arriving at Capt. Laureto's H.Q. Here they learned something of the organisation – they were told that in North East Mindanao there was a Lt. Col. McClish who was in command of the Guerillas in that area and he was able to communicate with Colonel Fertig who commanded all the guerillas on Mindanao. However it was some weeks before they would be able to reach McClish's H.Q. Passed from one friendly Filipino-American family to another they were amazed to find these isolated loyal Filipino and Americans prepared to suffer so much hardship and remain free in the belief the Americans would return. Capt. Laureto was able to maintain a watch on the Japanese in Davao as the organisation was linked by radio to the rest of Mindanao. Whenever the party arrived at a village or barrio they were entertained lavishly by the Filipinos – even though many were poor the presence of the Americans gave them hope.

Their destination was Medina and not far from a strong Japanese Garrison. However they eventually found the station at Anakan which was, in better times, a large logging establishment complete with miles of rail-road and a transmitter. It was here that Commander McCoy prepared a message to be transmitted to Fertig addressed to the Commander of Naval Forces, South West Pacific – and another message to Lt.General Sutherland, G.H.Q. United States Army in Australia.

McCoy's message stated: "Arrived after escape from American Prisoner of War Camp at Davao with three Marine officers – three Air Corps and . . . Artillery and two Sergeants, all captured on Bataan and Corregidor. Have extensive information regarding Corregidor brutalities and atrocities with extremely heavy death toll to war prisoners. Have some information on Davao Province. If practicable request entire party, plus two Filipinos who aided escape, depart here by next transportation."

The message to General Sutherland was sent under the name of Major Mellnik, Senior Army Officer of the party. After repeating the same facts as in McCoy's letter, it said: "Fifty percent of United States Armed Forces in Far East who surrendered in Bataan, are now dead from malnutrition and diseases. Remainder in various stages of beri-beri – dysentery – malaria and blindness due to vitamin deficiency."

These messages were the first reports of the condition of American prisoners in Japanese camps. The day was May 6, 1943.

It was about this time conditions in Jap POW camps started to leak to the outside world – however it would be several months before the Allies could make the allegations of Japanese brutality public as they were still planning to evacuate these officers from the Philippines.

Commander McCoy and Major Mellnik proceeded to Misamis where Fertig's H.Q. was located at this time. Here they learned Fertig had sent another message that McCoy and Mellnik have now arrived at Misamis. A reply came from G.H.Q. to their first message ordering the two men out on the first submarine. Their immediate reaction was what about the rest of the party?– well, they would have to wait. Fertig needed their skills to assist in the Administration of the organisation. It will be mentioned later that the Australians who could have contributed so much to help those at Sandakan were retained by Fertig. McCoy, Mellnik and Dyess were evacuated by submarine early July 1943.

It was Lt. Col. Mellnik who was to become one of the principal experts on Japanese POW Camps in the S.W.P. Command. He was sent to Washington to join the MIS.X., an organisation set up to recover prisoners of war and missing airmen. From late 1943 on, G.H.Q. began to study the problem of possible relief of those held by the Japanese. It seems the only action they could take now was to expose to the world the barbarous nature of the Japanese conduct towards POWs.

In the meantime the Japanese were now launching counter-measures against Misamis – their attack commenced on June 26,which shook the very foundations of Fertig's H.Q. A large reward was offered for his head but the Filipinos remained loyal; Fertig was chased out of Misamis back into Lanao with his friend Charles Hedges.

Lanao was the stronghold of the guerillas, however Fertig was uncertain whether the main transmitting station should remain there; after long talks with Hedges and Bowler he decided to establish his H.Q. in Aguson Provinces under the protection of McClish's command.

The Japanese at this time decided to hasten the construction of the airfields the POWs were building at Kuching and Sandakan in British North Borneo. A further 1,000 British and Australians, known as 'E' Force, were despatched in April on the old Dutch ship, the 'De Klerk'. The British contingent of 500 under Lt. Col. Whimpster were left at Kuching while the Australians under Capt. R.J. Richardson were loaded on to a small cargo vessel, the 'Taka Maru'. It had just off-loaded a consignment of cement and the POWs had to contend with cement dust for the rest of the journey.

On this ship were a number of officers and men in separate parties who had met up during the voyage and discussed their escape plans. One group comprised Lts. Blow, Gillon, Capt. Steele and Lt. Wagner, all determined men who had been planning their escape since becoming POWs. They had taken the opportunity of being placed on this draft because it seemed to offer the best opportunity. The other group was led by one Pte. R.K. McLaren who was to become one of the most famous of all Australian guerilla fighters in World War II, and his mates Rex Butler and Jim Kennedy. McLaren had previously escaped from Singapore only to be betrayed by the Malays. This time he wouldn't be trusting any Malays.

During the voyage Steele and Wagner approached the officer in charge – "Let's take the ship over! There are only 20 guards – we can handle them and we'll head for the Celebes!" Richardson wouldn't agree to the proposal, he said, "It's my job to get these men home." Later Blow said if they had known of the Filipino Guerillas operating on the Island it may have been different.

While off loaded at Kuching for a few days they learned from internees in the camp that the Police Force at Sandakan was loyal and named Corporal Koram, 142, as a particularly reliable contact.

On April 15 they arrived off Berhala Island at the entrance to Sandakan Harbour – Berhala, with its steep sandstone cliffs covered in thick vegetation, and in the foreground was what was previously the Quarantine Station,which until recently had been used to house the civilian internees who had now been moved to Kuching. Here the men were disembarked on to barges for transportation to the jetty at the camp. They were marched to an open area where they were lined up and ordered to place their belongings on the ground to be inspected by the Japanese. Their main interest seemed to be writing material; Rex Blow was able to conceal his .38 pistol he had acquired in 1942 at Adam Park Camp.

Following the search, the Commander of the Sandakan Camp – Captain Hoshijima – arrived. The Camp now contained approximately 2000 British and Australian POWs; Captain Hoshijima stood on the stage and told the POWs they would remain on the island a for a short period, cutting timber for the construction of their camp, which would be on the mainland. He warned them he was well qualified to command and knew all about their ancestral background. As Hoshijima continued exposing his knowledge of Australians as thieves and scoundrels Blow murmured to his mate, Miles Gillon, "We won't be staying around with this bastard for too long!"

The POWs settled in what appeared to be idyllic surroundings and were fortunate in having the same police guards as the internees had had which made contact comparatively easy.

Discussions took place between the two escape parties to ensure their plans were co-ordinated so both parties would leave the camp at the same time – if one made a premature departure the chances of the other parties would be much more difficult. They were all placed on working parties which gave them the chance to reconnoitre the island. McLaren spotted canoes tied up at the Leper Station and said to his mates, "We'll have those!" Wagner was able to make contact with Cpl. Koram who promised every assistance and explained that the Filipino Guerillas were operating in Tawi Tawi, only about 100 miles away, and one of their men would be coming to Sandakan in a kumpit soon and they would arrange to take them there.

For three weeks they remained on the island and were allowed to swim daily along the beach. Blow, a former champion swimmer and Wagner, a strong swimmer, were conspicuous by distance swimming and remained in the water longer than the others. Word came from Koram the Japs proposed moving the POWs to the mainland.

That night, June 4, both parties left the camp – Blow and Wagner swam out and confiscated the canoes and brought them into the beach for McLaren's party of Butler and Kennedy. They were met by very angry lepers who explained by actions they were taking their livelihood away; they depended on the canoes for obtaining fish. These appeals fell on deaf ears – one canoe had been sunk to indicate to the Japs the whole party had left together. The five boarded the canoe and dropped Blow and Wagner by the cliff then headed down the coast to freedom – they arrived at Tawi Tawi on June 14.

Here they met Col. Saurez, Commander of the 125 Regt., and informed him there were four officers, one O/R and natives waiting on the island for Cpl. Quadra to pick them up. In the meantime Koram kept in touch with those remaining and provided them with food. It was a long three weeks, sweating it out waiting for the Japs' patrols to cease before it was safe for Quadra to come anywhere near Sandakan.

On June 24 Koram arrived again and informed them arrangements were made for them to leave Berhala at 2000 hours on June 26 and they arrived off Tawi Tawi on June 29.

They were invited to join the 125 Regt. and given tasks within the Regiment. In the meantime Suarez sent a courier off to Fertig's H.Q., now on the move on Mindanao, to inform him 8 Australians had arrived having escaped from the Sandakan POW Camp.

Back at the Camp, when the guards reported there were 7 men missing, the Sergeant slapped the Privates and when the Sergeant informed Hoshijima there were seven men missing the Sergeant got a severe thrashing; and then Hoshijima was in a spot – he had to inform the powerful Kempe Tai the men were missing. Hoshijima had already been embarrassed at Sandakan when the Kempe Tai caught McKay and Harvey attempting to escape; they were shot on the spot and not allowed to be buried in the cemetery.

Captain Ray Steele was appointed to an Administrative position; Blow and Gillon were put in command of a battalion which comprised a band of cut-throats, and Wagner was happy to be doing what he liked best – Intelligence – and in no time he was visiting adjacent islands to get the lay of the land. They were warmly received by the Filipino people.

It was not till after Captain John Hamner arrived in July 1943 with Lt. Young to establish a radio station that Suarez was able to contact Fertig's H.Q. direct.

Tawi Tawi was first occupied by the Japs in 1942, their main garrison in the area was Jolo where they maintained an air garrison. Occasionally patrols would visit the island – burn a few buildings – commit atrocities – which deepened the resolve of the Filipinos to fight on.

From the end of July 1943 the Japanese would have been aware of the radio signal emanating from Tawi Tawi. Apart from those at Sandakan there was a concentration of U.S. POWs at Palawan; they were taken from Luzon in 1942, to construct an airfield at Puerta Princessa.

Personalities were beginning to merge with common interest. The first Bn. of Tawi Tawi led by Blow, Gillon, Butler and McLaren decided to subdue a band of pro-Jap Moros.

After a couple of days they learned their first lesson in dealing with the Moros on their own ground – they were ambushed. Rex Butler was killed and Miles Gillon got his left side peppered with an assortment of hardware. Despite their losses they killed the Moro leader, Datu Mohammed, but were unable to recover Butler's body. This loss hurt McLaren, who vowed he'd make up for the loss of his mate. During the fighting one of the Filipinos deserted, his body being found later minus arms.

It was not until September 1943 that the first message was received by H.Q. S.W.P. requesting names and details of the Australians on Tawi Tawi and also the Americans who had escaped from Palawan. Later, Capt. Steele requested Capt. Hamner to convey a message to H.Q. S.W.P. requesting the evacuation of the sick members of the A.I.F. party. Hamner never sent the message, it was a matter for Suarez to sort out with Fertig who contacted the main network station. It was unlikely any unauthorised message would have got past him.

In October a message advised that the Australians had permission to proceed to H.Q. 10 Military District if they so desired. Charlie Wagner commenced hunting around for a suitable kumpit and crew.

Arriving in Mindanao in November the party made their way north through various guerilla contacts – they were not far behind the Japanese who for the second time had devastated the area. It was not surprising that at this time support for the Japs was down to about 5%.

The sick members of the party were sent off to hospital to recuperate and within weeks both groups crossed Panguil Bay, near Illigan, where they were ordered to await further orders as it was known the Japs were assembling a force at Misamis for further raids in the area. These came a few days later.

The Australian officers reported to Lt. Col. Hedges, C.O. of 108 Division, whose H.Q. was generally located on the eastern side of Panguil Bay. At this time Col. Fertig had been forced to move his H.Q. to Aguson, leaving Hedges in control of Lanao. Capt. Steele and party reported to Hedges who gave them a cool reception, considering them a burden at the time and extra mouths to feed. However when that night the Japanese invaded Illigan, the Australians immediately volunteered and became involved in the fighting which continued for the next few days; it was during this episode Charlie Wagner was killed by a sniper. This loss left the Australians a bit shaken and more determined.

After losing 50-60 men the Japs withdrew and the guerillas moved back into what was left of their area. One of the Japanese objectives was to find and destroy the radio station. The Australians decided they would like to remain with the Americans, the officers being appointed to executive positions.

The two sick men were ordered to be evacuated. All the Australians were promoted and these were later confirmed by General Blamey in a message through Fertig's H.Q. Within a few weeks before the evacuation another message arrived from Fertig's H.Q. that one officer was to return to Australia to provide intelligence on all events since the fall of Singapore. No one wanted to go – eventually Steele was nominated as the Senior Officer. He received orders to proceed to Aguson when transport was available.

The Australians distinguished themselves and displayed leadership qualities fighting the Japs. They must have impressed Hedges considerably as fighters for he asked them to dinner and during the course of the evening invited them to stay and fight on. In fact, they had already decided between themselves they would like to join the Americans.

Tor Knudsen, a Norwegian, was at Hedges' H.Q. at the time and remembers their arrival. "They made a big impression on me. They were brave and determined to do anything to win the war. Right after they arrived the Japanese attacked our forces and I had several opportunities to see the Australians in action. Although they adhered to the time-honoured tactic of the guerillas, 'hit and run', they changed it completely. They certainly hit the Japanese soldier whenever they had a chance and they did run also, but not away from the scene of action but after them! Trying to get as many as possible of them!"

The Guerilla Organisation throughout the Philippines had grown considerably; special radio transmitters, manufactured in Australia for easy transportation by submarines, were supplied and by late 1943 there were stations operating on the major islands of the Philippines including about 40 on Mindanao with the principal transmitter close to Fertig's H.Q. in Aguson province.

The Japanese were obviously worried about the radio traffic which they must have calculated meant more submarines were servicing the guerillas. Up to this time fleet submarines en route to a mission would drop off a small party of technicians and 3 or 4 tons of stores – not very much for an expanding guerilla army.

MacArthur for some time had requested the super subs. be put at his disposal – these were the NARWHAL and NAUTILUS – first commissioned in 1930 they were 371 feet long and an extreme beam of 33.3' and a displacement of 1000 tons above the fleet submarine. The complement 8 officers and 80 men. Both carried 26 torpedoes and had 10 tubes – their surface speed was 17 knots, submerged they made 8 knots. Since the outbreak of war these subs had been used to put Marines ashore and also used to evacuate civilians in the South West Pacific.

By 1943 the two giants were showing their age and occasionally black smoke when they were under pressure. The NARWHAL was ordered to report to H.Q. S.W. Pacific in October 1943. Arriving at Brisbane she underwent a refit to prepare her for the guerilla run; torpedos and facilities were reduced creating extra space so she was ready to carry 92 tons on her first mission. Commander Parsons would be returning on this mission with a party of nine officers and men. Lt. Commander Frank Latta took the NARWHAL north – the plan was to land half the cargo at Mindoro, only some 75 miles from Manila, and the balance somewhere on Mindanao for Fertig.

The NARWHAL had taken the Pacific route through Surigao on the northern tip of Mindanao – until now most subs had taken the western route through the Celebes Sea. Soon after midnight the watch reported contact with two ships astern – believed to be Destroyer escorts – he was more convinced when the ships put on speed. Latta put all engines on line and increased speed – the enemy opened fire – he called for more speed. He elected to remain on the surface, trusting there would be no breakdown in the engine room – they may decide to fight it out with his 6" deck guns. Down below in the engine room somehow the engineer nursed the four engines and prayed – the rev counter registered a few knots over the limit – subjected to flares from the enemy the huge sub manoeuvred on the surface to avoid shell-fire. During this chase, the engines – 'Matthew', 'Mark', 'Luke' and 'John', were racing as they never had before; the engineer spoke to the Bridge and said, "Captain if we don't slow down we won't have any engines left! Latta replied immediately over the voice-tube, "If we slow down we won't need those damn engines!"

The NARWHAL outran the Japs and in the process the Captain became confused as to his position in unknown waters; however, Parsons was able to identify a well-lit town on Negros – there were not many; they proceeded on to Mindoro. At their chosen landing site there was a patrol boat in the area which did not detect the sub creeping into Paluan Bay and Parsons and his men went ashore in the darkness. The NARWHAL cleared the area to await Parson's signal. Later, a rubber boat flying the correct signal was observed – the NARWHAL surfaced and the boat stood out to meet her. She went into the bay and moored alongside a schooner flying the Jap flag. They unloaded her cargo and she left for her next destination, Butuan Bay in the mouth of the Aguson River where Fertig's H.Q. was now located, when the sub surfaced off the bay a small boat with Fertig aboard went out to meet her. It was on this occasion the NARWHAL got stuck on a sandbank which must have caused great consternation, however, after sallying her she cleared and tied up at a pier deep inside enemy territory as the local band played "Anchors Away". An incredible accomplishment just a few miles from a Jap Garrison – After several hours the NARWHAL took on evacuees including Major Steele, Kennedy and Wallace of the A.I.F., and headed for Australia. A signal From G.H.Q. advised him to rendezvous with another pick-up off Tawi Tawi en route.

On 5 March 1944 the NARWHAL sighted the signal of Captain Hamner, Captain Latta was not to know the drama which had been going on over the past weeks – and he did not know that Hamner and Lt. Cain had taken refuge in Borneo months earlier with the British party under Major Chester (code-named PYTHON). Both their groups were operating in areas where a large section of the population was pro-Japanese and only about 25% who could be regarded as friendly – while the rest were negotiable.

Hamner was first aboard, Major Jinkins presented written authority from the officer in command of PYTHON, Major Chester, for Captains O'Keefe, Broadhurst and himself for movement to

Australia.

The usual procedure on the guerilla run was for the local natives to provide fresh fruit to the submarine – a boat came alongside loaded with green coconuts and the fruit to be presented to the crew but crew members commenced throwing stores on the deck before the coconuts could be unloaded. The boats available were not sufficient to carry the assigned stores to Major Chester and Colonel Suarez, so Capt. Latta made the sub's rubber boats available to ferry the stores ashore.

Jinkins had earlier arranged a fire to be lit on the landing beach to guide the stores boats ashore. The unloading was taking longer than anticipated and much of the stores were on deck when radar detected an incoming vessel at 8500 yards – all guns were manned – the crew were ready with their carbines. Capt. Latta took immediate action to clear the decks of people, closed all hatches and headed for the open sea; the NARWHAL remained on the surface to charge her batteries; altogether three enemy ships were identified but during this time effort was made to recover as much of the stores remaining on deck as time permitted before submerging. One of the destroyers opened fire on the NARWHAL as Latta gave the order to dive – Armed with two 6" guns and with a top speed of about 17 knots she could handle small surface ships effectively and she was so large it was not unusual for passengers to be unaware of other passengers on board – and that was the case with Major Jinkins not knowing of three escaped 8 Division POWs from Sandakan, now dressed in U.S. uniforms, also being on board.

After a few dives to avoid aircraft, the NARWHAL reached Darwin on March 11, 1944, and later went on to the Task Force Base at Fremantle.

Major Steele, wearing an American uniform with a Colt on the hip, would only have been identified by Brigadier Rodgers, the Director of Military Intelligence. He was taken to H.Q. where he met General Blamey and in the time allowed gave a history of the events since the fall of Singapore. This was the first reliable briefing Blamey had. Steele was later flown to Brisbane where he was de-briefed by Rodgers and senior members of his staff. Later, with Wallace and Kennedy, they were transferred to Melbourne where the process continued; a lengthy exercise of going through Nominal Rolls until they were satisfied there was nothing else to be learned. Sworn to secrecy, the three were given leave.

It was not long before W.O. Wallace broke his Oath of Silence and started talking about those left at Sandakan. Wearing his old Unit insignia he was approached by many people seeking news of their loved ones. In fact, Wallace was to embarrass those now considering if anything could be done to give relief to those back in Sandakan.

When Steele's report reached the Services Reconnaissance Department, the seed was sown to plan a rescue operation. It was Top Secret and code-named Kingfisher –

It was at this time Brigadier K. Wills was appointed Controller of Allied Intelligence Bureau, an Organisation especially created earlier in 1942 to co-ordinate all intelligence gathering and subversive operations against the enemy. The principal section responsible to A.I.B. was the Service Reconnaissance Department dominated by British officers principally concerned with operations in South East Asia. There were many other sections controlled by the Navy and Army operating in the South West Pacific. The Dutch demanded their own organisation which was known as Netherlands East Indies Intelligence Services – this was controlled by A.I.B. however they sought and gained direct access to G.H.Q. It was logical for A.I.B. to request the Dutch to provide intelligence on the N.E.I. for forthcoming operations.

In Australia the A.M.F. commenced forming and training the 1 Aust. Para Battalion. It drew its volunteers mainly from A.I.F. Units who were impatient for a different type of action and many of whom had seen service in the Middle East. By late 1944 they were ready for action and had undergone specialist training which included a possible rescue of POWs located behind Japanese lines. Also well advanced was 'Z' Special Unit which attracted a similar type of volunteer except that these men were trained in small groups and never were to know what the other parties were training for. Their training encompassed parachute drops in enemy territory, learning Malay, the most common language spoken in South East Asia. Most of these parties only spoke Malay – they were sworn to secrecy and were subject to intensive tests to qualify for such tasks.

Long-range aircraft became available for them to move deep into enemy territory. From 1942 most of S.R.D. operations were concentrated on targets closer to Australia where intelligence of the type required could have been gained by air reconnaissance without the risk and high cost involved of inserting gound parties. The story of S.R.D.'s embarrassing failure has been described elsewhere, their parties were compromised in Timor. Unaware of this for some time they continued with food drops. (At the end of the war the Japs sent a signal of thanks for the aid.) These failures were kept from G.H.Q.

The British participation in this theatre seemed to have irritated the Americans. It was not until Wills became Controller did relations improve.

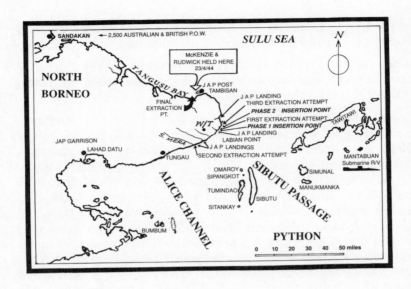

U.S.S. NARWHAL   *U.S. Navy*

Chapter 3

Early in May 1943 Allied Intelligence Bureau (A.I.B.) proposed to place an intelligence gathering party into the east coast of Borneo. This proposal was put to General Headquarters (G.H.Q.) and soon approved because it fitted into the Guerilla radio network now being established throughout the Philippines. The plan was to establish Observation Posts over the Sibutu Channel and seek contact with agents along the east coast up as far as Sandakan and down to Tarakan.

It seems when this plan was conceived no consideraton was given by the A.I.B. as to the possible reaction of the Japanese in the event of any of the Commandos being captured or their presence becoming known so close to Sandakan Prisoner of War Camp containing some 2500 British and Australians.

It is understood the Commandos were instructed that if any of their number fell into Japanese hands and if they were visible they were to be shot rather than be subjected to interrogation and torture.

Two parties were inserted into this area. There were no losses until Phase 11 was inserted four months after the first insertion. The Japanese captured three men.

This Chapter tells of the movement of this party, code-named PYTHON, of their success, their losses, their eventual evacuation, the hell of being depth-charged in a submarine, and the Japanese reaction which ultimately would add great pressure on the prisoners of war at Sandakan.

Captain F.G. Chester (later Lt.Colonel, and better known as 'Gort') was appointed leader. He had spent many years in Borneo as a planter and at the outbreak of World War 11 offered his services in the British Army where he first served under General Heath in the Abyssinian Campaign. He possessed great knowledge of Borneo and claimed to know many Chinese merchants who represented the hard core of commerce throughout the country. His second-in-command was Captain Broadhurst, formerly of the Malayan Police Force, who spoke Malay fluently. There were four Australians to make up the party: Captain E .O. 'Paddy' O 'Keefe, Lt. L.J. Woods, Sgt. L.L. Cottee and Sgt. F.G. Olsen – both Signallers.

This group volunteered for enlistment in 'Z' Special Unit. Lindsay Cottee was formerly a Signaller with the Armoured Division and when the threat to Australia passed, after the Coral Sea battles, he was seeking more action – he found himself training with this group.

He recalls: "We assembled our stores in Melbourne and then loaded them on to a R.A.A.F. Dakota and flew across to Perth. On arrival, the U.S. Navy collected our stores and we were taken by U.S. Navy Staff cars to the Adelphi Hotel, which had been taken over by the U.S. Navy Officers for a Leave R. & R. while they were in Perth.

"After three days as guests there, on the third night we boarded the U.S.S. KINGFISH, which was moored in Fremantle Harbour. It was then we were told our destination was Borneo, it came as quite a shock. Outside Fremantle we played hide-and-seek with a Dutch destroyer and could hear the propellors as they passed over us. When they made a successful run over the crew of the submarine would fire a small smoke bomb to indicate that they had made a successful pass.

"We then proceeded to Exmouth Gulf where we topped off the fuel tanks from a Dutch tanker then on to Lombok Straits, we had to go through at night on the surface as there is a very strong tide rip which makes it difficult for a submerged submarine to get

Labian Point. Python Area.   W. Jinkins

35

through quickly and they said they could see the lights of the Japanese airfield.

"The submarine then proceeded to the Celebes where they laid fifteen mines. We arrived at our destination alongside Borneo on the 5th October 1943."

Captain Lowrance of U.S.S. KINGFISH described the event: "During daylight of October 6, a submerged reconnaissance of the entire area was conducted. Approaches to within one and one half miles of the beach were possible. No activity was noted so the decision was made to land the party at about 2000 hrs that evening.

"At 1900 hrs the ship was surfaced and stood out to sea. The sea was glassy calm, no wind, and the moon was about one quarter but covered by cirro cumulus clouds. Visibility was limited.

"At 1930 hrs course was reversed and preparations started for the disembarkation. All equipment was brought up on deck through the after battery hatch and stacked just aft of the bridge superstructure. In all there was 97 pieces. The four boats were inflated by using the ship's air supply.

"When within three miles of the beach, battle stations were manned and the ship was trimmed down so that the deck was within about two feet of the water. The approach was made by using soundings and radar ranges. When the range to the beach was about 1700 yards the ship was stopped and unloading was commenced. At 2015 hrs the first rubber boat left with Captains Chester and O'Keefe. At 2115 hrs the remaining three boats (one being towed) left.

"The progress of the party was followed until they were seen to be quite close to the beach. We had arranged signals so that in case the landing attempt did not come off we would try to recover them. In the absence of any signal we were to assume that the landing was successful. At 2330 hrs when no signals had been seen we stood out to sea and resumed our patrol.

"On the following day a submerged patrol was conducted in this vicinity with an approach to within two miles of the beach, but no activity was noted. All indications pointed to a landing without incident (or accident) and a successful concealment."

Sgt. L. Cottee: "Olsen and I were in a six-man rubber boat fully loaded with stores and other members of the party were in two-man rubber boats. The rubber boats were loaded on the deck of the submarine and when we were ready they lowered the submarine into the water so we could float off. The noise of the compressed air leaving the vents nearly blew us off the submarine – scared the daylights out of us!

"As we paddled away the tide rip quickly pulled us apart, our boat being more heavily laden we couldn't keep up with the other two, so we tied the boats together and paddled ashore in that manner.

"When we arrived at the beach we unloaded the stores and, because it was raining heavily, we turned the large rubber boat upside down and huddled under it. We didn't get any sleep that night – we were cold and wet and Chester produced a flask of rum and gave us all enough to keep us warm. The next night we were settling down for some sleep on the edge of the jungle next to the beach, and we were amazed at the hundreds of fireflies flying around underneath the undergrowth, giving the area a dull glow bright enough to see one another. We carried food sealed in four gallon tins, sufficient for eighteen days per man. It consisted of dried mutton, dried onions, dried potatoes, dried carrots, rice, milk, tea, coffee, salt, pepper, sugar, curry powder, chocolate, compressed dried fruit, tobacco, cigarette papers, matches, Army biscuits, etc. etc.

"We set up our main radio camp – to make it easier for us to find our way back and forwards to the beach we blazed a trail, cut a nick out of the bark in each tree in a straight line, so we could find our way through the undergrowth. This meant we went up and down over the ridges and in the gullies it was very thick and dense with lawyer vine and growth, whereas up on top of the ridges it was only light growth, light forest. After making a few trips I noticed the animals preferred to go round from the top of the ridges where it was easy walking and, although it took a little longer to get to the beach, we went much quicker following the ridges. Lawyer vines are a very strong vine covered in hooks and when we would walk into them they would rip our clothing and cut our skin, and it was very difficult to get ourselves out of them. We were greatly troubled with leeches, every time we'd stop and some of the chaps would have a smoke, they would be busy putting the hot end of the cigarette onto the leeches to make them drop off; every night when we would take off our boots our feet would be covered in blood from the leeches that had been active around our ankles and dropped off."

During the first few weeks the party reconnoitred the area where they were going to establish their camp and watcher station, became accustomed to the sounds of the jungle animals and the regularity of Japanese patrols. After settling down, Chester made contact with the Tawi Tawi guerilla station.

Captain Hamner, U.S. Army, first received orders in May 1943 to take an Intelligence party on the Sulu Archipeligo. His mission was to establish three radio stations, Basilan, Jolo and Tawi Tawi. Its principal task was to report shipping movement in the Sibutu Channel, the major passage used by Japanese shipping. All their reports would have been transmitted to General Headquarters, South-West Pacific.

Captain Hamner arrived at Tawi Tawi where he established a station to assist Lt. Col. Suarez of the United States Filipino Forces. Hamner had already distinguished himself by escaping from the Philippines in a native boat and returning by submarine to set up radio stations. While at Tawi Tawi he met the eight Australians who escaped from Sandakan and who were later ordered to H.Q. of the 10th Military District in Mindanao on October 23, 1943 for evacuation.

Soon after Chester arrived there he made contact with Hamner, who then joined them in Borneo. Using Hamner's boat, Chester visited a number of islands in and around Tawi Tawi where he met an old friend, Lt. Valera, now under Suarez' command. With Valera's assistance, he appointed a number of Agents and was able to meet up with Lim Keng Fatt who associated with Dr. Kwok of Jesselton.

Scene on Tawi Tawi.   W. Jinkins

Returning to his base for a few days he decided to visit Col. Suarez to request Lt. Valera's transfer to Borneo to make use of his vast knowledge and of his contacts. Valera had worked for many years in British Borneo.

Lindsay Cottee said of Lt. Valera: "He spoke good English and often entertained us when we were bedded down in our hammocks at night. He had a young lad with him who helped him sail the boat; I watched this lad kill a small shark with a piece of wood. He cut the shark up into strips and dried it in the sun. Their food consisted mainly of fish and tapioca root. On one of the excursions when Chester, Valera, the lad and myself were crossing the Sulu Straits (Sibutu Channel) we sailed into a Japanese convoy. Chester and I climbed under the floorboards with the stinking fish, while a low flying Jap aircraft flew overhead, close enough for us to observe the pilot and gunner through the cracks of the floorboards. We told our crew to wave madly and appear friendly; we sailed past the convoy and were close enough to see the Jap soldiers lining the rails and even hear them talking. We were all relieved when the convoy finally passed by."

At this time a plan was approved by G.H.Q., without consulting

Sgt L.L. Cottee on board U.S.S. Harder   *L.L. Cottee*

the parties concerned, to set up a scheme for the development of British North Borneo Intelligence. The Americans believed the British had no interest in such an undertaking, and showed no interest in the proposal. Hamner believed the scheme was feasible but wanted to return to Australia for medical reasons before being involved.

There was a vast network of radio stations in the Philippines and none on the Borneo coast, seems to confirm the British did not want the Americans involved in former British Colonies.

During the period Captain Hamner and Lt. Cain were with Chester's party, considerable valuable information was passed on to G.H.Q. from the radio station. The Japs suspected this activity and often sent aircraft flying low over the area, searching for signs of life.

The PYTHON party was established in a strategically important and sensitive area; most of the Japanese shipping moving south to the oil ports of Tarakan and Balikpapan sailed through the Sibutu Channel within view of their look-out.

During this period Chester was able to organise his agent to visit Sandakan; however, he was not to know until Hamner arrived that Ray Steele, Rex Blow and the rest of the party would be able to provide the most up-to-date intelligence from that area; furthermore, while Lt. Charles Wagner was on Tawi Tawi he compiled a most comprehensive summary of intelligence from Singapore to Tawi Tawi. There was no advantage for POWs at Sandakan by the presence of PYTHON, in fact, events would prove the Japanese regarded their presence as a threat to Sandakan Airfield and POW camp.

A second party under Major Jinkins, and comprising Lt. A J. Rudwick, Warrant Officer A. Chew, Sgt. D.G. McKenzie, Sgt. W. Brandis and Sgt. Neil embarked on U.S.S. TINOSA, commanded by Captain Weis, from a base in Western Australia on 10 January 1944, and on 18 January landed successfully complete with stores. Owing to insufficient space in the submarine, some of the stores, which included arms, ammunition and medicines intended for Dr. Kwok, had to be left in Australia. A short time after landing, Sgt. Brandis disappeared in the jungle. He became lost on his first day and for some weeks wandered in the jungle, eventually being found struggling along a beach near Kampong Atiam by Osman Panjang. Brandis was in a pitiful condition and starving and could not stand upright. He was naked and indicated by sign language that he had been in the water for three days. He indicated that he wanted food and was kept and fed at Kampong Atiam for a few days; the native chief, Mandor Alam, heard the Japanese knew of Brandis' presence so he went to them and confessed he was sheltering a white man. A native, Jaria, had previously informed the Japanese. A Japanese Police Inspector and two Police boys arrested Brandis at Tambisan where he was handed over to the Kempe Tai who had arrived from Sandakan.

The Kempe Tai was under the command of Warrant Officer Kuroda, his interpreter was Isamu Miura. Kuroda said Brandis was dressed in clothing provided by the Japanese as he had lost his own while using them as a bouy to swim a river when he had become lost soon after his arrival in Borneo in January. He disclosed he had come from Australia by an Australian submarine to join other Australians who were already in Borneo for the purpose of transmitting information to Australia on the movement of Japanese shipping and armed forces. Kuroda was anxious to find out the precise number of Australians and where they were located. Brandis was only able to remember that where they had come ashore, there a keel of a boat under construction.

After the interrogation was made the Japanese took Brandis to

Sgt. William Brandis WX.16743 'Z' Special Unit. GinGin W.A.
Executed by Japanese 30.12.44   S. Neil

where he thought they first landed. This search continued for a few days, then the next day they found the remains of a camp site but there was no sign of the commandos; they then returned to Sandakan with Brandis. The Kempe Tai and some of Capt. Takakuwa's men continued their search between Tambisan and Tungau for some weeks without success; one night during this search the Japanese opened fire on their own men believing they were the Australians, killing one of their own soldiers and wounding several others. In the meantime back at Sandakan the Kempe Tai started to work on Brandis continuously, evidence suggests the interrogation was carried out by several interrogators – it was common Japanese practice to maintain physical pressure on prisoners.

Soon after the completion of the compilation of Brandis' interrogation the report was sent off to 37 Army Headquarters at Jesselton. While Major Chester would have sent off a signal to S.R.D. Headquarters in Melbourne advising them Brandis was missing – this signal forewarned Headquarters the PYTHON Party would be in for special attention by the Japanese.

The Japanese were now aware there were a number of Australian officers already in Borneo equipped with transmitters; orders came from the Chief of Staff to intensify the search as a matter of urgency. It was also at this time the Japanese reorganised their Borneo Garrison into the 37 Army and moved their Headquarters from Kuching to Jesselton.

On 16 February 1944 a company of Japanese landed at a point one mile south of the Nyamok River. Stan Neil remembers: "The look-out was located on a platform up in a very high tree overlooking the Sibutu Channel, sometimes on a clear day we could almost see Tawi Tawi. Len Cottee and I were on duty after an early breakfast, we had

Japanese Destroyer sinking in the Sulu Sea.   W. Jinkins

just settled down when we saw a tug boat come around the bend towing a barge – then another and another – there were several we didn't wait to count. We shinned down the tree and reported back to Chester who was leisurely cooking breakfast on a fire. The smoke marked our camp precisely – they had us pinpointed. The party quickly dispersed to the jungle and observed the Japanese come ashore and assemble; it was not long before they found one of our food dumps and we watched them, through a telescope, rifling our gear. They were highly amused when they found a pair of scantees I had brought along as a souvenir from my girlfriend." and Len Cottee heard one of his mates say: "Bugger it! they've got my set of false teeth!"

The Japanese made a recce of the coast in that area and departed again two hours later. On the following day, 60 Japanese landed at the mouth of the Nyamok River, 2 miles south of Labian Point and 400 yards south of one of the coast watching posts. PYTHON hurriedly moved camp to the Tenagian Kechil River, about 4 miles further north. By now it was evident the Japanese were on their trail; this was further substantiated by information received from agents that the enemy knew there were white men on the mainland.

Because of Jap pressure it was decided to evacuate to the west coast; with this end in view, Lim Keng Fatt was sent on 17 February to confer with Kwok's successor and make the necessary arrangements for the reception of the party. His boat was to return to the east coast, pick up the party and transport them over to the west – Lim Keng Fatt never returned.

In the meantime it was decided to evacuate Captain O'Keefe for reasons of ill-health, with Captain Broadhurst and Major Jinkins, back to Australia by the submarine which was to bring up the remaining stores. On the night of 17/18 February these three, accompanied by three members of the party, left for Tawi Tawi to make the rendezvous with the submarine. Lt. Valera accompanied the party to bring back the stores.

Although the party leader reported that the rendezvous chosen, Mantabuan Island, was insecure, Jinkins claimed the Controller A.I.B., Colonel Roberts, refused to pass this information to U.S. Navy and the rendezvous was not changed. The evacuation party accordingly made the rendezvous on the date indicated, but as the recognition signals were not displayed at the correct place, no contact was made with the submarine. The party waited as arranged until 27 February, when the activity of the Japanese patrols forced them out of the area.

After this unsuccessful rendezvous they returned to Tawi Tawi, choosing a new rendezvous on that island. Contact was made with Australia, the new rendezvous was agreed to and pick-up arranged from 3–6 March. At this time, while proceeding to the rendezvous, Cain pulled his .45 and threatened Jinkins, saying, "You're not going without me!" Those present seemed taken by complete surprise by Cain's action and watched Jinkins walk up to Cain, speaking quietly and confidently, saying, "We're not going anywhere without you but I'll have that gun." Having disarmed Cain, the .45 was given to one of the other Americans; Cain was already under great stress.

On March 5 contact was made with the submarine, the evacuation party went on board and the off-loading of stores into native boats began. The U.S.S. NARWHAL was accustomed to meeting large numbers of friendly natives in Mindanao who provided numerous boats and crews for unloading stores, however, the position in Borneo was far more risky, as many of the natives were pro-Japanese and the unloading party was restricted to trustworthy personnel; therefore the procedure of unloading here took longer. But unfortunately the work was interrupted by the arrival on the scene of Japanese destroyers which approached to within 3000 yards of the NARWHAL. The Captain ordered unloading to cease and put to sea. Lt. Valera was on board when the submarine submerged and was also brought to Australia with the other three members of PYTHON party. The stores off-loaded reached Tawi Tawi, but due to Japanese activity on the mainland the boat was unable to deliver them to PYTHON. This placed a great strain on Chester's party as they had used their food supplies to assist Hamner's party over the past few months.

Some of the supplies left on the deck were later recovered, the Japanese then claimed the sinking of the submarine.

Unbeknown to Jinkins, Major Ray Steele, escaped POW of the 8th Division, was on board being sent to Australia to be de-briefed on all events since the fall of Singapore and carrying with him Lt. Wagner's intelligence reports up to the time of his death. This information would have downgraded any information PYTHON party had accomplished on the situation of the POWs at Sandakan. It is not known what part of the submarine they were in as Hamner would have recognised Steele – it is most unlikely either party would have come in contact with each other in such a large submarine where movement was restricted.

During this time Japanese patrols had the balance of the party who were still on the mainland of British North Borneo well on the run. The enemy landed 12 patrol parties in two days between the Mera and Tenagian Kechil Rivers. The food and stores dumps were

Left: Sgt. Donald George McKenzie WX.40238 Mentioned in Despatches. 'Z' Special Unit. Executed by Japanese 30.12.44 from Mount Hawthorn W.A.   Noel McKenzie

Right: Lieut. Alfred John Rudwick VX.102007 'Z' Special Unit Mentioned in Despatches. Executed by Japanese 30.12.44. Ballarat Vic.   S. Neil

found by the Japanese and an hour after the W/T Station had been moved to a new position the old site was occupied by the enemy.

Stan Neil: "About this time the Japs had us on the run, they landed not far from where we were camped; anticipating trouble we had planted stores in various localities. Lt.Rudwick and Sgt. McKenzie were sent to guard the rentis which was our main track to our base. Alex Chew and myself were sent to relieve them and of course when we got there there was no sign of them at all – so we started to call out until we realised the Japs may have been close by, so we returned to base.

"Unlike other parts of the jungle in this locality, sounds carried some distance; we figured Rudwick and McKenzie were just yarning when the Japs got wind of their presence, crept up and jumped them. After that we were all very careful about sound. It was a bastard of a place – we could not shoot wild pigs or game for food. The only natives seen in the area were a few Malays on their fishing boats who had seen us, I guess they would have reported our presence to the Japs."

On 22 February 1944 a Japanese party under Lt. Ota left Sandakan to carry out another search of the Nyamok River area. After spending a few days in the locality they were reinforced by Lt. Okamoto and another thirty soldiers.

In mid-March a rubber boat was discovered together with empty cans having contained food and clothing, also some containers still full. The Japanese concentrated their search in this area as they located the marked trees leading to the tracks to the camp site. Interpreter Miura later gave his version of the capture of Lt. Rudwick and Sgt. McKenzie: "Whilst walking through the jungle on one of these tracks we saw McKenzie carrying an automatic weapon followed by Rudwick who was carrying a pistol – the Australians were on their way to seize the Japanese food dumps – they were ambushed by Kempe Tai and other soldiers.

"At first they would not talk, but after a few days when they thought that their friend was safely away, they talked willingly. Sgt. Matsuii Kioshi of the Kempe Tai with me as interpreter, questioned them about the number in the party etc.

"As soon as they had been caught they were asked for the location of their camp, but until they started to talk they did not lead us there. When finally they did show us the location their friends had escaped. They left behind four wireless sets and one empty set.

"We returned to our camp by the sea-side that night, and Kempe Tai made rough interrogations, asking from where and how the Australians had come.

"Kempei Mukai took three Australian captives to Sandakan Kempe Tai where they were interrogated by Kuroda.

"When Rudwick and McKenzie were caught they wore green jungle long sleeved shirts, and green long trousers. Rudwick wore rubber canvas boots but I do not remember what McKenzie wore on his feet, I don't think they wore belts. They had no labels around their necks or in their pockets. Rudwick was wearing an olive coloured hat, but I think that McKenzie was not wearing any.

"Rudwick had nothing in his pockets, but McKenzie had a black covered note book about 2½" x 5" in which he had taken notes regarding the movements of Japanese ships. The notes covered the tonnage, direction in which proceeding, speed, time and dates of the ships which he watched from the coast. He said that he sent wireless messages containing these particulars to his main camp in the jungle from where it was transmitted in secret code to the Headquarters in Australia.

"I remember that, after McKenzie and Rudwick were brought to Sandakan Kempe Tai, the three Australians were photographed individually in the clothes they wore when captured, but without any of the captured military equipment. I think this photo was taken to send to Army Headquarters with the interrogation reports. Just before the Australians were sent to Jesselton another similar picture was taken, this was attached to the Kempe Tai report to 37 Army Judicial Dept."

The U.S. Navy signalled Task Force 71 at Fremantle with instructions to order submarines to a rendezvous; three attempts by USS BLUEFISH, HADDO and REDFIN failed to extract the party, consequently Captain McCollum, U.S. G.H.Q., requested Major Jinkins to investigate the reasons for the failures.

An attempt was made by Chester Nimitz, Jnr., in USS HADDO. He

Commander S.D. 'Sam' Dealey of U.S.S. Harder during 1944 – Lost off Luzon, August 1944.

waited close offshore for two hours, he was not to know the commandos did not have a boat, so he continued his patrol. Later, when interviewed by Major Jinkins, he asked why didn't they float a log out Jinkins replied: "You don't know the sharks around there!"

Lindsay Cottee: "We tried to obtain a pick-up by the USS REDFIN – we had carried our large rubber boat down to the beach and we had erected a white sheet just before dark so they could find what part of the coast we were on. We waited, and the first indication that something was wrong was gunfire, a fight took place between REDFIN's crew and a Japanese patrol boat. We realised that our pick-up had blown and we wouldn't be leaving Borneo that night so we waited until dawn and then we heard Japanese coming ashore and we took off into the jungle as fast as we could, none of us looking at our compasses and after about half an hour we found we were almost back on the beach again, we turned around and used our compasses and headed inland. Not long after we heard a Jap calling out thinking we were some of his mates crashing through the jungle and he was trying to attract our attention. We took off so fast and exhausted ourselves, after about a quarter of an hour we just sat down and got our breath back and then we got into a small creek and paddled up this creek for quite a way so as not to leave any footprints or marks for the Japanese to follow us. The rubber boat had been abandoned at the beach and we never came back to find that again."

Stan Neil: – "We were a long way from the pick-up point and we travelled overland in the jungle for two days or more until we finally came out at night – there were six of us and I was last in the line covering for us as we walked along the edge of the ripples of water to cover our tracks – we had our jungle boots tied round our necks and we had distributed the weight of the food between us – I had the radio and the others had the food. We were going along and we came to the Sungei Mera river – how were we going to get across without a boat – it must have been a pretty crazy sort of arrangement. On the left of us the moon was coming up and it was just like a ball of cheese – it was a wonderful night. The six of us were going along in single file with Gort leading when suddenly a challenge – Gort stopped and said, "That's not Malay that's Japanese – run!"

"We all turned round and instead of me being last I was in front and I ran for dear life along the bloody beach, of course I didn't know what the other fellows were doing – I thought they were behind me but they were smart – they went for the jungle and I was left out there on my own running in the bright moonlight! I looked around and thought I'd better get up in the jungle too so I started to get up along the beach running and I could feel the heavy machine

U.S.S.Redfin.   *U.S. Navy*

gun and rifle fire – light machine guns – they were really trying to hook into me because they could see me easy enough and they were getting pretty close because they hit a stone or a bit of sand and it stung me in the leg and I thought I was shot. I fell down on the sand and I thought I'm not going to die here without putting up some sort of fight so I cocked my gun and stood up and I shouted Fire! and I nearly shot my toe off! I couldn't see anybody else so I jumped into the jungle and I threw the radio off too which had the crystals in it. Then they set up a machine gun and they started to rake the jungle from the beach with machine gun fire. I stumbled through and got about half a mile – I'm puffed out, buggered, frightened and hungry – I stopped – I heard a bit of movement and I thought it was a wild pig then I heard this movement again so I called out, "Who's there?" and it turned out to be Olsen, so we were then on our own. I had a little bit of condensed chocolate and I asked him if he had any food but he said no, so I broke the chocolate in half and gave him half and that was all the food we had and off we went to find our way back to the Base Camp which was over two days' away. We walked and we walked and we got hungrier, we didn't meet up with any of the others. I remember going up a river and on the bank we came across the remains of a Japanese patrol stop, they had thrown their scraps of dried fish on to the fire and we got stuck into those, then we started to get scared because the Jap patrols were handy. I always reckoned afterwards that if I wanted to die it would be from hunger because eventually your mind just goes blank. You would forget to do things – suddenly I'd remember that I had left my belt off with my pistol, gun, compass and things and I would have to go back and find it. Finally though we found our compatriots and I will never forget when we walked into the camp there they were all sitting round and instead of them being pleased to see us one of them said – "For Chrissake!" he said, "Where the bloody hell have you been!? Now we'll bloody well have to re-arrange the rations!" Of course they had written us off and they each had got a bit of extra food and they were not a bit pleased to see us at all! That's what happened on the Sungei Mera pickup."

After Major Jinkins returned to Australia on the NARWHAL he learned of Chester's request to be extracted because the Japanese were now on their trail.

Following Capt. McCollum's request the investigation was duly carried out into the cause of these pick-up failures and revealed they were due to the fact that submarine crews lacked local knowledge and were not specifically trained for such work and did not possess suitable equipment; furthermore it was useful being able to speak the local language.

A plan was then submitted and subsequently approved by Admiral Christie, CTF 71 whereby Major Jinkins and one other operator, Sgt. Dodds, should be allowed to attempt extraction of Chester's party.

The coast watching resulted in a total of 88 enemy shipping movements being reported during the whole operation. These reports would have been processed by A.I.B. – much of the information reported was already mentioned by other sources – code-breakers, W/T from Tawi Tawi and submarines.

It was unfortunate that the misunderstanding between the parties led to the foul-up regarding the rendezvous appointments and the lack of boats for the removal of stores. Major Jinkins was later critical of many aspects, including the fact Captain Hamner talked too freely to evacuees on the submarine about his activities in Borneo, which affected the security of members who were still ashore. He subsequently reported: "Captain Hamner of A.I.B. was heard to have said, during conversation with several of the civilian passengers, that he had been working in Borneo, he had also given them the impression he was an Intelligence officer. His role in the Philippines was known to most of these evacuees whom he had met in his tour of this territory. Steps should be taken to check this officer's conversation, also that of Lt. Cain, in Australia, regarding PYTHON operations."

Jinkins was not to know Rudwick, McKenzie and Brandis were in Japanese hands when he expressed concern about Hamner in his report; he was also reporting: "The possibility of a very careful and searching interrogation of Lt. Valera by a Department other than S.R.D. should not be overlooked and steps should be taken to ensure this officer's status in Brisbane.

"Having been supported by Major Chester for 3½ months, they know a considerable amount about his work and the agents and areas which he has covered"; he reported further on Captain Hamner, "Both are inclined to talk about the task they have done to any person caring to listen."

The USS HARDER, under the command of Capt. Sam Dealey, was given the task of taking Major Jinkins and Sgt. Dodds to Borneo to undertake the rescue of Chester's party.

All stores and gear were loaded and the party left Fremantle on 26 May 1944; a full rehearsal of the rescue exercise took place in Exmouth Gulf, this was considered a great success and they got under way, arriving off the pick-up point on 7th June 1944.

En route to Borneo the HARDER ran into a convoy of three empty tankers and two destroyers heading to Tarakan for a refuel. One of the destroyers picked the submarine up and charged her. Dealey let it get within 1100 yards then fired three torpedoes – the MIUAT SUKI blew up and sank. Dealey gave chase, making an end around the convoy; he submerged to radar depth and prepared to attack. A second destroyer peeled off and charged HARDER. Dealey let it get within 1200 yards before firing six bow torpedoes – all missed. Dealey then went to 300 ft. to evade – a new diving-plane operator misread his instruments and took HARDER to 400 ft. by mistake, as a result Dealey lost another opportunity to attack the convoy and turned back for Sibutu Passage. At 11.43 he sighted another destroyer, allowed it to get within 650 yards then fired three torpedoes at five second intervals – all three torpedoes hit HAYANANI. He then went full speed ahead with hard right rudder to get out of the path of the destroyer. Dealey later recorded: "At a range of 300 yards we were rocked by a terrific explosion, believed to have been the destroyer's magazine. Less than one minute after the first hit, and nine minutes after it was sighted, the destroyer sank tail first."

The HARDER was then the target for the sister-ship of the destroyer and 17 charges were dropped in the next two hours. Dealey returned the periscope and found two more destroyers, then another one, then a line of eight! – feeling he had worn out his welcome he went on to a point north of Tambisan Island, where he made contact with the party.

Major Jinkins reported on the rescue operation:

"At 1900, 8 June 1944, two folboats were made ready in the forward torpedo room and all accessories assembled ready for passing through the forward torpedo room hatch to the deck. The submarine was under way on the surface making 1/3 speed on batteries toward a preselected position approx. 6,000 yards north of

U.S. Navy

U.S.S. Harder, off Mare Island Navy Yard Feb. 1944

the shore rendezvous.

"At 2055 hrs. the canoes were passed topside. Jinkins and Sgt. Dodds with assistance of the submarine's crew, V.L. Dallessandro, TM1C and W.F. Young, TM2C, completed the assembly of the canoes which were loaded. After a final checking of bearings and range the canoes were launched and they began paddling shorewards.

"The night was calm and slightly overcast with a smooth sea; at about 600 yds. from shore, contact with the submarine was established and she was informed the light signal to shore was about to be flashed.

"A white light was flashed directly on the compass bearing ashore, a pause of a few seconds and the light was again flashed on the position ashore. No reply. The light was then moved in an arc....to cover the immediate vicinity of the coast and then returned to the first position. This time a light flash was seen from the shore at the exact spot. The letter 'V' for Victor was flashed ashore to which was replied 'Y' for Yoke; a 'B' for Baker was flashed ashore and the commentary of the proceedings was given to the submarine by radio. Indication that the canoes were then proceeding ashore was

Sgt. Stan Neil on board U.S.S. Harder 9.6.44

53

also given the sub. The radio was secured and the canoes paddled inshore to approx. l00 yards from the mangroves. The water, at this stage, was less than six inches deep with a soft, thick, mud bottom. Radio communication was again opened up with the sub. and light contact with the shore party re-established.

"Voice contact was then established with the shore party and an open circuit maintained with the submarine. The first challenge, "Who are you", was replied to by, "Gort". This reply was recognizable by the voice as being that of Major Chester. The second challenge made was, "Is Alex with you?". The answer, "Yes" in WO. 2 Chew's voice was heard. Chew was then asked who his Platoon Sergeant was (he having had only one). The reply was, "Doddsie". This reply was correct and proved beyond doubt that the party ashore was the PYTHON party."

Stan Neil:
June 6th
> Pick-up date from 6th June to 13th June. Arrive at RV 12.30 pm 6th after 5 days forced march. Feeling pretty well done in. Have food till 11th but no water. RV swamp with mud up to the knees have hammocks slung over mud. Affected by tide so that water is couple of inches under the old bot when full tide. Mosquitoes and sand flies murderous. Altogether a depressing place. Food consists of strictly rationed dehydrated tack. Can light no fires so eat it raw with no water. It swells the tummy but makes you dry as hell. Expect signals between hours 6pm and 12 o'clock midnight so all mount lookout sitting on logs watching hopefully. Mossies and sandflies make it hell. No signs so we retire for night 150 yds through the black stinking mud.

June 7th
> Sitting about this depressing place all day with no water getting us all down. Eating the food raw and dry doesn't help any either. Still tonight should be the night we are all confident for we have radioed the sub that all is clear. Go to our usual logs and silently stare at the ocean hoping against hope for signal lights. 11.30 pm thru 12 no signal so we go to bed. Can't sleep too so thirsty.

June 8th
> Alex and I decide that water must be got so we decide to leave at 7am. I have no boots left and Alex's are one size too small and rooted. He has lost both his big toenails through wearing them. Nearest water is 5 hrs march away through swamp and neepa make it by 12.30 to find it brackish and affected by tide.

Fill the 4 gal. food tin and set straight back. Must be back by nightfall. My feet are cut to pieces so Alex has to carry the water. Lose a lot as the lid is not a good fit. Arrive back about 6.30 with about 3-3/4 gals and ration two mug fulls to each person. That will last 24 hours. Take the swampy taste out of the water by adding soluble coffee. Not bad to drink.

7p.m. Alex and I join party at the coast and anxiously peer out to sea. Not so confident tonight as we expect it to come off on the 7th.

9 p.m. Alex and I go back into jungle for smoke. Discuss best plan should pick-up fail. Have worked it out previously and go over our plans again.

10 p.m. Gort calls me back into jungle for talk. He is really worried now. Says if pick-up comes off and we get out safely he is going to recommend me for commission. Thank him but not interested in commissions just now. Wants to know what Alex and I have planned should the pick-up fail. He like the rest of party are dead scared that we will leave them. They all come at different times to ask us our plans. I give Gort the same answer as to the rest. Just that we haven't discussed it fully yet. Gort talks of taking his 'L' pill or surrendering and I leave him with less chance of that commission than when the conversation started. He is eating above his rations also.

11.45 p.m. Alex and I go back to jungle for another smoke. We are really worried. Lloyd calls us out and says that he thinks we should all offer up a prayer. It is decided so we all join in The Lord's Prayer. Alex and I return to finish our smoke.

11.55 p.m. Light sighted right on the beam. We return sig. It's them alright. Alex and I dive for our chocolate ration and start eating. Gort goes a bit hysterical and swears it's the Japs "trying to lure us out"

9th June

12.30 a.m. It's Bill and Stan Dodds alright in 2 folboats. Low tide so we have to go 150 yds through mud to get to boats. After 4 or 5 steps we are all hopelessly stuck up to our thighs and can't move. Fred digs himself out and helps the rest to extricate themselves. He gets bright idea of crawling on hand and knees which proves quite successful but slow. 30 mins to do the 150 yds. I'm the only one with my weapons. Determined to get them out. Others throw theirs in the mud. Our prayer was surely answered.

Left Sitting: Major W. Jinkins, Warrant Officer A. Chew, Major Chester, Lieut L. Woods.
Standing Left: Sgt. L.L. Cottee, Sgt. Olsen, Sgt. S. Dodds, Sgt. S.Neil.

L.L. Cottee

1.15 a.m. Bill puts an outboard motor on folboats and off we make for sub. Owing to shallow water (she's waiting in 3 fathoms) 6 miles is the closest she could come in.

2.15 a.m. We are guided out by Radar from sub. Sub in sight and we are soon on board. We are all thrilled. Climb down Fwd. hatch to Fwd. Torpedo Room where clothes are stripped off us and a hot shower follows. The Yanks are marvellous. Can't do too much for us. Everyone you pass hands you a carton of cigs., a toothbrush or clothes. Have a wardrobe full in no time.

3.15 a.m. Captain has Wardroom set up with royal feed. We assemble there where after 3 whiskeys (George V Scotch) we set about steak and eggs, strawberries and cream and many other fancy American dishes.

Am full and tired by now so retire and am soon asleep.

5.30 a.m. Diving alarm sounds followed a couple of seconds later by great crash. Aerial bomb lands 20 yds away and we were only 60 feet down. Sub. lurches the lights flicker and I get really scared. Another further away this time. We trim out at 250 ft. and all is quiet. Ruins my sleep so I go and eat. Eat – can't stop eating and drinking coffee this day."

Lindsay Cottee: "The morning following our rescue, the diving alarm sounded – I woke up and smelled the fresh food that had just been baked while we were on the surface during the night and, as the fellows from up on the outer deck came inside, I asked them what was the problem and they said apparently there was an aeroplane coming at us from out of the morning sun and that's why we dived. Eventually three bombs landed close to us but they didn't do any damage."

As the USS HARDER headed north to the Philippines on the 9th June, Stan Neil

"5.30p.m. Been under water all day. Two destroyers coming our way at 30 knots. Captain gives order "Battle Stations without the alarm" – I'm to get my first taste of underwater warfare with the submarine's deadliest enemy, the destroyer, and I'm dead frightened. Hear the Capt. give the orders "Fire one" "Fire two" etc. until he releases 4 fish. Breathless silence while we wait for the explosion, 3 sec. 4 sec. 5 sec. The two terrific explosions and the Capt. reports one destroyer going down. 3 sec. later another explosion and the other got it fair amidship and explodes immediately. The action is over in less than 2 min. We dive as the other destroyers come in to depth charge us. We are forced down to 400 feet. Being depth charged is a nerve wracking experience. We sit at 400 feet while the destroyers go over and over us letting them go about 10 a min. All fans and machinery are turned off so that they cannot pick us up with detectors and at the end of 4 hours the air is pretty foul. To walk to the `head' is a terrific strain on the lungs. One is breathless after 20 yds. We are all made to lie down and not talk to conserve oxygen. All is quiet by 12 midnight so we surface and beat it. That makes four destroyers to this Captain's credit this run, he has been out 2 weeks so far. A record for any submarine.

10th June

4.30 a.m. Depth charged and bombed by planes again. Am too tired and don't even know we have had it. Just as well perhaps. **5 o'clock p.m.** Been down all day owing to planes and destroyer activity. Batteries running very low. Excitement as Captain is called to periscope for nothing less than 3/4 of the Japanese fleet comes into view, 4 Battleships, 8 Heavy Cruisers, 6 Aircraft Carriers and auxiliary craft including 15 odd Destroyers. To everybody's amazement the Captain orders "Battle Stations without the alarm". He is going to attack the Japanese Fleet, just one little submarine! Explains to crew that he wants a battleship and tells them of the risk then starts to give his orders over loud speaker. Three explosions before we fire a fish. Another sub. has scored 3 direct hits on one of the battle waggons. They are 10,000 yards from us and making our way so the Skipper decides to carry on. All is ready to fire fish when destroyer escorting fleet spots our periscope and heads straight for us at 37 knots measured by sound gear from the rpm of screws – intending to ram us. With zero angle on the bow the Skipper fires 3 fish to connect with the destroyer which is carried on by its own momentum towards us. We dive to avoid it but hear it go straight overhead and 5 sec. later explode. The explosion almost caused us to sink. Knobs came off instruments and doors – we were all thrown to the floor. Fuel lines broke and started to fill the crews mess and water rushed into crews' quarters fwd. To top it off the destroyer escort attacked us with charges. We went down to 490 feet to silent running again and I prayed as I never have before and really meant it too. By midnight we were on top again, making a total of five subs Dealey had sunk in a fortnight. We have 5 fish left too."

Lindsay Cottee;
"....the Captain announced over the loudspeaker system that he

58

had spotted an aircraft carrier and he said we'll see if we can sink it. However there must have been planes flying around and his next announcement was that we had been spotted and there were two destroyers heading in our direction. The next I knew was that we felt the three torpedoes being fired, they are fired with the compressed air and a sort of shudder goes through the submarine as they leave; immediately the torpedoes are fired the crew all look at their watches to check the time the torpedoes are running, after a certain time if they miss their target they automatically blow up, this is a safety measure because they have been known to go off course and come back and be quite dangerous to the submarine which fired them. We could hear the destroyer's propellors coming towards us, as we dived sharply we could hear her go over us then there was a terrific explosion as the torpedo hit and the ship blew up which sent everybody to the floor of the submarine, water started pouring in in places and the crew were running around caulking various places, shutting valves and opening other valves, and we could hear a mighty roar through the submarine, it was a crackling sound like a violent thunderstorm, the crackling became similar to steam being released into a bucket of water but amplified millions of times and making a tremendous sound, evidently the destroyer's boilers were belching steam into the ocean as she sank.

"The submarine was tossed around like a cork and everybody was struggling to get off the floor after being thrown down. I was sitting near Stan Neil in the Mess Quarters and he told me after that I was as white as a sheet and I said, "You're pretty white yourself!" One of the crewmen got down on his knees and he had his hands together praying, they couldn't shift him during the two hours that we were being depth-charged.

"We dived to 450 feet and this particular sub – this particular type of submarine – was tested to go for 300 feet. At the 400 feet depth the hull continually creaked and cracked and groaned, we could tell there was tremendous pressure on it. In the Control Room they had a bathosphere and the stylus tracked a short horizontal line on its lamp black card as round the 200 ft. level as we dived, so the Captain brought the sub. up to this warm water current which, at this level, helped deflect the enemy echo-ranging. We removed our shoes, the air conditioning was turned off, everybody was warned to be very quiet and even not to raise their voice, with no air conditioning during that two hours and such a lot of electrical cabling in the submarine made it very hot and everybody was dripping with perspiration. We spent a very anxious two hours with propellors coming and going and depth charges getting louder and receding. It was quite an experience, rather hard on the nerves. We eventually surfaced when it was dark, however the Captain was pleased to see a lot of wreckage on the surface of the ocean.

"One night we were on the surface and we pulled alongside a sister-submarine, the USS HADDO under Captain Chester Nimitz, Jnr., the Captains were able to talk to each other across the water; later on our Captain took his submarine in close to a breakwater so he could stick his periscope up and look into a harbour and see how many Japanese ships were there, we spent some time looking around, poking round the area, and then we headed back to Darwin, having run out of torpedoes.

"When we arrived at Darwin on 21 June, the crew took out all the pennants of all the ships they'd sunk, there were 21 that day and most of the crew that were not on duty came up on deck as we cruised into harbour." (The USS HARDER and her brave crew with Captain Sam Dealey was later lost off Luzon on August 24, 1944.)

Stan Neil: "We arrived by the train from Adelaide; when we got into Melbourne we noticed a large number of senior Australian officers on the platform – we thought General MacArthur might have been expected. When the train stopped all these people converged on us, shaking our hands – we received a welcome which I never understood. Later we were booked into Carlyons

U.S.S. Harder going into Darwin
W.Jinkins

60

Hotel opposite the Station where we were de-briefed and caught up with our mail while Major Chester caught up with the other ranks."

PYTHON was a great success – the party had been inserted 2000 miles deep inside enemy territory and successfully reported on the movements of enemy shipping over a period of several months.

After Major Chester was withdrawn no attempts were made to replace PYTHON in that area nor any joint effort made to cover the Tawao-Sandakan area. It was proposed the intelligence gathering in that area would have been left to Lt. Valera (who was caught below on the NARWHAL when the Jap destroyers were sighted). Now Chester was to make other arrangements, which failed. He was disappointed in losing Lt. Valera's services who was later to go into Luzon before MacArthur's assault.

A G.H.Q. Report stated: "The failure of the Hamner mission is disappointing but not discouraging......" In returning to the Philippines at the Commander-in-Chief's bidding and making the long and hazardous journey to Tawi Tawi, remaining there until actually driven out by occupying forces, Hamner displayed courage and loyalty deserving of the highest commendation and should not be blamed for the ensuing failure of the project to which he was committed.

Finally, Captain Hamner was blamed for the failure of co-ordination of work in the area. When he arrived back in Australia he was not recognised for any Award such as Parsons and Smith had been after their first mission to the Philippines and Jinkins reported the area too hot for submarines to be risked. Both Chester and Jinkins informed A.I.B. Tawi Tawi was in imminent danger of being invaded again – Colonel Suarez and his Filipinos never were caught – and the Sibutu Passage remained the demarcation line of British and American interests.

* * * *

Albert Kwok, sometimes referred to as 'Dr.' Kwok because of his work in China with Chiang Kai Chek's forces, returned to his preferred country, North Borneo. In 1940 and later in 1942 he commenced contacting small guerilla groups and bringing them together under one Command. At this time the Japanese were beginning to put pressure on the Chinese community to contribute funds and manpower to be conscripted into the Japanese Forces for the defence of the Sulu's, this action precipitated premature action against the Japanese and on 10 October 1943 Kwok's guerilla forces attacked police stations in the Jesselton area. The uprising was brutally put down – the Kempe Tai massacred hundreds of Chinese; Kwok's assistant and principal contact was Lt. Lim Keng Fatt, formerly a merchant from Kota Kinabulu (Jesselton), who joined the Filipino Guerilla Forces at Tawi Tawi; it was here he met Chester and informed him of the plans in hand for the establishment of the guerillas on the west coast. Lim Keng Fatt became one of Major Chester's principal "mail men" during 1944; Chester claimed to have provided him with a large sum of sovereigns – and at the time he was not to know the Jesselton uprising had failed.

During March 1944 Lim Keng Fatt wrote a number of Reports which reached Col. Suarez on Tawi Tawi in August 1944 and later Australia via Leyte G.H.Q. These extracts portray the harshness and cruelty of Japanese rule and the difficulty of commando parties operating in the area and also underline the great problem escaping POWs faced running gauntlet through often hostile territory. Lim Keng Fatt returned to the west coast with arms provided by Col. Suarez and the cash to buy support – it was at this time he was murdered by Bayau near Tuaran.

Lim Keng Fatt:
"There was a complete change since I left the country last October when condition was still very good. Since the start of the guerilla attack on 9 October 1943 Japs had adopted a policy of threat and intimidation of the population by burning all Chinese farm houses and looting of all their belongings. Dusun kampongs suffer the same should such kampong supply Chinese with food or accommodate Chinese civilians in the hiding or guerillas. From rough estimate as told me by our guerilla members who are now with us, that not less than 300 Chinese farm houses and about 100 Dusun kampong houses were burnt down and looted by Jap. soldiers. These houses were mostly belonging to civilians and non-combatants and all foodstuffs, clothing, cooking utensils, crockery and farming implements were either destroyed or looted, making lives of these poor sufferers very miserable.

"With all kinds of business – buy and selling, particularly foodstuffs – in the hands of Japanese monopoly it increases the hardship for the poorer class of civilians to secure foodstuff, as prices are very high on account of Japanese profiteering. The whole population is against this action but no one dares to oppose openly as a slightest complaint will produce trouble and will be arrested and beaten or slaughtered by Japs. Dusun paddi cultivators suffer no less as they have to plant paddi, not for their own consumption, but must be given to Japs monopoly at a very low price, leaving only a very small portion scarcely sufficient for themselves till the next harvesting.

"At present rice is being rationed, just imagine in a rice producing country, and fresh vegetables are now getting scarce, the Japs have destroyed our farming implements, they control our blacksmiths and no one is allowed to make any knife or tool without written permission. Chickens and pigs were either let loose or killed when the Japs burned the Chinese farm houses, no one is allowed to buy or sell any animal and the Japs take all the meat available for themselves. The people are not allowed to go to sea for fish unless they have special licence and special permission, these are very hard to get. Material for clothing is almost unobtainable. But in the interior of the country where the Japanese have not yet been garrisoned rice, chickens, eggs, pigs and cattle are still obtainable. I cannot buy coconut oil or sugar and would advise you to bring enough stores for your needs."

"Since my return here Japs are daily hard on my trail making any movement from camp impossible, therefore, contact for military intelligence information will be very slow unless good money can be spent to employ good and reliable agents. Japs are employing not less than 30 to 40 agents in places such as Inanam and Mengattel where formerly infested with guerillas, thus prevented me from visiting my own home in Inanam. For the present I do not intend to make the visit which will be dangerous for my family and myself, I need clothes and medicine very badly but must go without for the present.

"I am wanted by Japs with offer of $5000 reward to anyone getting me alive or dead, the reward is the highest ever offered as Japs consider me the most important man who has not yet surrendered to them.

"My family is made prisoner and is not allowed to get out from the house and all my property has been confiscated and been sold to a Japanese concern now running a brandy distillery which was run by me and my partners before. Japs have been seeking information from my wife of my whereabouts, with threat of death to her should she hide the truth. They use all kinds of tricks and way and means to find whether I have actually returned to this country, as they are in doubt of the report which was given by Dusun during my landing in Telibong. The report stated that one Chinese with machine gun and four Sulus with side arms were seen passing on the main road to Telibong rubber area.

"Japs spent good sum of money to employ spies and agents to stem our guerilla movement and to catch those who had not surrendered to them, salary of these agents from $100 to $350 per month with special bonus, from this you must understand that we must spend similar amount to counteract them. I intend to use very intelligent men with salary from $200 to $400 per month, but the money given by you is scarcely sufficient as I had to keep the same for buying ration for our men. However, I will try to secure agents if it can be made to pay their salary on your arrival."

Lim Keng Fatt reported he had met two men, former inhabitants of the Mantanoni Island, and they told him that a Sulu man by name Buangchi, an inhabitant of Manganoni, went to South Ubian, Sulu Islands, to buy sugar and trade in Jesselton; when he was caught by Japs and heavily beaten, in order to secure his release, he passed the following false information charging that the Orang Tuan of Mantanoni was harbouring eight Chinese who were in hiding. On this information Buangchi was released to accompany ten Jap soldiers to arrest the Orang Tuan.

The Japs went in one launch and the Orang Tuan and twenty Sulu men were arrested and brought to Jesselton where some of them were massacred and some imprisoned. On account of this Japanese atrocity all the inhabitants of Mantanoni were enraged, they sent a Petition to the Jap Commander at Jesselton that they would prefer to be all slaughtered rather than to live under unfair charge.

On receipt of this Petition the Jap Commander sent fifty soldiers, equipped with two machine guns, in two launches and, on arrival at the Island the Japs proceed to burn all kumpits and boats to prevent the inhabitants from escaping. On seeing this happening, all the men, women and children themselves lined up, all women dressed in their best with all jewellery they have and the men with their weapons of pujaks and parangs ready for the affray. Japs opened machine gun fire and rifle fire and fighting ensued, resulting in the killing of 20 Jap soldiers and the Commander. The number of Sulu people killed was 126 men, women and children. All houses on this Island were burnt by Japs, with the exception of the Mohammedan Mosque. There were now only a few women left and living on the Island, without any means of transportation to get away; those still living were the ones who fled to the hill to hide themselves.

On March 28, 1944, Lim Keng Fatt sent a further report: "I advise we are still in the same camp to date, not able to get away to the sea side as intended as we could not get any one to buy us a small boat. Our runner, Kong Chow Siong, had just arrived and introduced to me an old man – Pang Sang – whose service will be useful to spy and locate a native boat for us to steal and to guide us to get away safely. This man is engaged at $100 for the job, plus cost of the boat to be given to the boat owner. I expect to get away in or about the end of the month at the earliest.

"I failed to secure the service of Mr. Chong Luk Chong, a salt-maker on the Malawak coast, this man was formerly a rubber inspector. Although there would be no difficulty or any risk involved should this man be willing to assist us to buy a boat on account of his business position but he simply refused without any reason, he even scolded our runner whom was sent by me to negotiate; this man knows me personally, and therefore I shall blame him for not giving us the helping hand.

"The most difficulty after stealing the boat is securing sufficient foodstuffs, natives on the coast have been severely warned by the Japs not to sell any foodstuffs to persons not possessing a pass from them. To do so, which means to say that they are trying how to cut guerillas or unwanted person from getting food.

"There is strong rumour current at present that Japs have caused all the able-bodied men (Sulu) arrested, the number already arrested amounted to some 300 men from the surrounding Islands of Danawan, Palau Sulu, Palau Sapit, Palau Ordar and Mangkalum Island. Japs accused these people as rebellious and they will be sent to Kuching for internment where they will be trained to fight against us. There was also rumour that there was fighting a few days ago between native policemen in patrol and some six kumpits full of Sulus, well-armed. There were some 10 native policemen killed and over 20 wounded, the casualties on the other side unknown.

"There was also a rumour about Japs capturing some Sulus, some 25 automatic pistols and two cases of cartridges smuggled into Galisan the concession of Pangiran Fatimah, therefore Pangiran Fatimah was arrested about a week ago, including 30 Chinese.

"Japs are still pouring reinforcements of troops into Jesselton by numbers of 30 to 40 men weekly, according to some reliable sources. These reinforcements were transported in small naval wooden boats, usually used in fishing. At present Japs concentrated more soldiers in Tuaran, they are being transferred from Telibong. Rumours often say that Japs have more than 1000 men in Jesselton alone, this I do not believe, the actual strength according to reliable source is not more than 500 all Japs, excluding some 150 natives and Japanese internees, the latter are used for guarding the airfield at Tanjong Sur.

"At present much work is being done by Japs to construct tunnel shelters on the hills opposite the airfield, to shelter planes in case of air attack. Many small attap and Kajang houses have been constructed on the Likas Plain for the purpose of evacuation.

"Japs are using planes to patrol the sea very often now – early morning, midday and afternoons, the precaution is on account of submarines being often sighted and ships being attacked too often on the East Coast of Northern Borneo.

"The three hundred .45 calibre pistol cartridges which I took with me are not useful at present as the pistols were surrendered by Kwok to the Japs, if possible, bring over pistol of this calibre. Please do not forget to bring with you plenty of side-arms, hand grenades, submachine guns, as we need them to convince the natives and for our secret movement in the country. All our men are suffering from malaria therefore please bring more quinine will you; I have to pay $30 for an ounce of quinine, which was bought for our men."

.... and that was the last A.I.B. heard of Lim Keng Fatt – and it was the last of S.R.D. operations in the Borneo area for almost a year. Much of the lack of initiative was placed with the then Controller of A.I.B., Colonel Roberts, who, in the words of a fellow officer, ".......... didn't get on very well with anybody – particularly the Americans."

Eventually A.I.B. was re-organised; Brigadier K. Wills was to take over as Controller and many of the smaller Sections were also pulled into line as the Organisation seemed to be getting too fat far away in Melbourne. Soon after Morotai was taken, Wills moved his H.Q. forward where projects could be placed before G.H.Q., thus avoiding the long channels of communication through the various Commands.

Success of the PYTHON pick-up by U.S.S. HARDER was helped considerably by having Major Jinkins and Sgt. Dodds on board to carry out the actual rescue, this convinced Admiral Christie's Operating Officer that the practice of taking specialist commandos on missions involving pick-ups could be beneficial to the U.S. Navy. As a result it was later agreed that six of Jinkins' men be trained for Submarine Guerilla Liaison.

Much could have been achieved during 1943 – 1944 by A.I.B. had there been less friction between the British, Americans and Australians. The British dominated S.R.D. were concerned with keeping the U.S. out of former British territories. The PYTHON operation in as much as reporting enemy shipping movements was a great success – much could have been done but Major Chester wanted no part of the east coast of Borneo – the U.S. were anxious to extend their coast watching stations into North Rorneo however there was resistance from the British.

S.R.D. failed to act to give the native population hope as

MacArthur was doing in the Philippines; while it is conceded Borneo was a lower priority a few messages of hope – even a promise – in the form of medical supplies could have worked wonders, however they chose gold as the means of winning the contacts over and this of course was not negotiable and attracted predators under the present circumstances. Drugs widely distributed in the area where parties were operating could have insulated the POWs and guerillas against the Japanese.

The Americans had recovered Japanese cypher books buried on a beach in New Guinea and after a quick translation they were able to establish where the strong points were located – this information facilitated General MacArthur's drive along the coast of New Guinea. Strong bases were by-passed and the Japanese could not predict where his forces would strike next.

While celebrations were going on in Melbourne over PYTHON' s return the back-lash was now being felt by the two thousand British and Australian prisoners of war in Sandakan.

The senior Japanese officers of the 37 Japanese Army Headquarters at Jesselton started to reassess the real significance of the presence of Australian commandos less than 100 miles from Sandakan where there was a large concentration of POWs who, at that time, were in a reasonably fit condition. The camp was located just 1½ miles from the airfield which was being constructed as a major staging field for medium type aircraft to reinforce their forces in the Philippines. The Japanese obviously considered the possibility of the Allies seizing this field with the assistance of armed POWs.

Orders were issued by Southern High Command at Saigon to the 37 Army and to Colonel Suga, Prisoner of War Administration at Kuching, to reduce the rice ration. This action was designed to render the POWs an ineffective force in the event of an Allied assault. Furthermore, a signal went to General Headquarters, Tokyo, requesting reinforcements to protect the airfield and also forwarding a report on the capture of the three Australian commandos. Orders were issued to send the 2 Battalion 25 Mixed Regiment under Captain Yamamoto, now in Manchuria, to Sandakan. The unit arrived in October and were soon established at the 9 Mile peg, just one mile west of the POW Camp and about one mile from the airfield, which was now nearing completion. Yamamoto later stated in evidence his duty was to construct defences to defend the airfield from Allied attack and to assist with its construction. Colonel Otsuka also received further reinforcements for his garrison.

By June, 1944 the first signs of tightening up and squeezing the

POWs was evident, apart from the ration cut. All men were searched as they came back into camp from the working parties – they were only permitted to bring back what they had taken out. Sensing a possible attack on the camp, Hoshijima cut off the electricity supply to ensure wireless could not be used.

A large, timber constructed, fortified machine gun pillbox was built between the old boiler house and the dairy farm, on a rise, with gun openings covering the camp area – the slots were beyond reach from the ground. Owen Campbell worked on the wood cutting party for this project. Guards were now increased around the camp and on all working parties. Natives were kept away from the prisoners.

At this time Hoshijima would invite the Camp leaders to his house for an evening meal – they would have to pass the accusing eyes of those serving a starvation stretch in the cage. Captain Cook would have felt those eyes as he walked by. Some of the men just commented: "Lucky bastard getting a feed!" Hoshijima, now established in the Wong's house, the basement of which housed several hundred bags of rice, was just not generously giving Capt. Cook and Capt. Mills (the British Camp leader) a meal – carefully selecting his English and pointing with his chopsticks he would try to test out and pry into the minds of his dinner guests to ascertain if there had been any contact with the outside world – their hopes of ending the war and, as Hoshijima claimed later, to maintain a friendly contact after the war – a most unlikely outcome! Hoshijima must have felt insecure and concerned as he heard the drone of the high flying reconnaissance planes now appearing overhead. He set about, on his own initiative, to increase the size of the vegetable garden and must have realised he would be held personally responsible for the condition of the prisoners. The orders from H.Q. strictly laid down the ration the prisoners were to get and it was this action which placed the prisoners in such a condition they would not be able to assist an invading force or escape to freedom. He travelled to Jesselton to seek an increase in the ration only to be told the ration scale was determined by Higher Authority and there was nothing the Quartermaster could do to assist. He appealed to Colonel Suga but was told he had no authority to countermand orders from Southern Command.

After June 1944 the vegetable issue was reduced to kangkong and some tapioca; there was no further meat or fish ration. The starvation program was under way when the first bombs dropped on October 14, 1944.

While the condition of the POWs deteriorated, deaths increased and coffin making ceased, Sticpewich observed the Japanese opening boxes of American Red Cross medicine for their own use while our men were beginning to die in great numbers because of the lack of quinine.

By September 1944, the earlier order reducing rice rations had been effective – Hoshijima was unable to supply the required labour to the airfield. He could not have things both ways – either a fit working force or POWs unable to assist the Allies.

There was no shipping available to move the POWs from Sandakan, the last had arrived in July 1944. The U.S. submarine offensive was now intensified to prevent reinforcements reaching the Philippines. Imperial General Headquarters ordered empty ships returning home to bring Allied prisoners of war who may be of some value in final peace negotiations. However disaster struck those chosen to go to Japan – between September-October 4000 Allied prisoners of war were lost at sea due to U.S. submarine action. From one shipload of U.S. prisoners, five survived from 1,800 – they managed to reach the China Coast.

The ration cuts rendered the men ineffective as a force of strength in just three months, a man who would have weighed 12 stone at the surrender of Singapore was now reduced to 8 or 9 stone.

As Christmas 1944 approached the P38 Lightnings would appear over the camp at precisely 8.30 a.m. Prisoners coming in from the airfield were stopped at the gate, from there they could see all the others who remained in the camp standing naked on the parade ground – a search was in progress, guards rifling through their huts and their personal gear. When the search was completed the workers were allowed into the huts.

Christmas Day was just another day – the only pleasure the POWs got was to watch a large formation of B24s put the airfield out of action; the Christmas Day raid gave them hope. Christmas dinner for the POWs was half an M&V tin of corn and rice mixed with dried fish and pork soup.

The trial of Rudwick, McKenzie and Brandis was about to take place. Earlier in September 1944 the three men had been taken by ship to Jesselton and placed in the old British Gaol. Here, the head of the Judicial Department of the 37 Army, Major Nishihara, having studied the Sandakan Kempe Tai reports, started to interrogate the three men. Nishihara spoke English fluently and had been a Judge at the trial of Capt. Lionel Matthews. He also supervised his execution. To understand what was going through Nishihara's mind at this time it is appropriate to read the the Judgement of the trial of Capt.

Matthews; translation of the trial is told to show their concern of what the POWs thought was a fairly harmless case of possessing a radio set in the camp. The Japanese believed otherwise and sought advice from the War Ministry and now, with information flowing from the PYTHON men, they would have linked the events together – up to this time they did not take repercussion against the POWs but now, according to the survivors, ration cuts were being implemented.

The Judgement: Five defendants, belonging to their respective Units, participated in the Greater East Asia War, taken prisoners by the Japanese troops at Singapore on 15 February 1942, and were being held in 1st Branch of Borneo POW Camp at Sandakan, East Sea, Borneo.

1. Defendant Lionel Colin Matthews, who had a hostile feeling for the Japanese troops even after surrender and dislike for the life of prisoner, was watching for a chance to escape.

Since arrival at the camp he worked in the attached farm outside the stockade every day. Around August 1942 he, taking advantage of relaxed watch, came to contact with Abin, a Dusan and Head of the Eight Mile Branch Office of Sandakan Police Station, several policemen under Abin, Matusap, a Dusan and watchman of attached ranch to the East Sea Provincial Agricultural Experimental Station, a Chinese farmer, Alexanderfan (Alex Funk) and several local natives. Although he knew that correspondence and contact with local natives outside the stockade were forbidden by order of Lt. Hoshijima Susumu, Chief of the Camp, about October the same year, he still continued contact with above persons and agitated Abin and others suggesting that those who assist the action of the defendants, prisoners, would warmly be received upon the resurrection of the British Administration. From the middle of March to July 1943, he, with continual criminal intent, selected the neighbourhood of the farm as a place of contact and secretly met with Abin generally once a week, and not only made him mediate correspondence between him and those outside the stockade but also met and consulted with the local natives.

About August 1942 he requested Alex Funk to draw maps of British North Borneo and Sandakan to use some day and received them. Then he was told by Alex Funk that there was a rumour that a large number of U.S. troops were stationed in Sulu Arch., and that they would shortly make a landing at Sandakan. He believed it would be possible and intended that in the event of landing of the U.S. and Philippine troops at Sandakan he would collect all the prisoners in the Camp, destroy it and co-operate with the troops. He asked and received from Alex Funk a pistol and six rounds of ammunition and arranged with him to notify him immediately by blowing a whistle outside the stockade in case the Allied troops made any landing. He asked Alex Funk to hand over a letter addressed to the Commanders of the Allied troops, in which he asked the rescue of the prisoners and enclosed a map of the environs of the camp. He told his intention to Policeman Abin and made him consent to hand over 5 rifles and 150 rounds of ammunition to the prisoners in case they started up. In order to report to the Allied troops in the event of their landing he tried to collect information concerning the Japanese troops. About the end of August 1942 he asked Alex Funk to draw a map of Sandakan and its neighbourhood, jotting in details of the strength and disposition of the Japanese troops and in December of same year he asked Maginal, a Dusan and Clerk at the Experimental Station for a map of the Station and the Camp and received both of them. In September 1942 he made Matusap persuade Lai Kueifu, a nurse at Sandakan Citizen Hospital, for a map showing billets and number of Japanese troops and residents there and obtained it. Whenever he met with Abin......he got information concerning the removal of the Japanese troops, and Englishmen and Americans detained in the Camp, the movement of Japanese fleet and ships in Sandakan Port and methods of supplies to the Japanese residents in Sandakan.

About November 1942 prisoners Weynton and Richards in the Camp secretly constructed a radio set and listened to a broadcast from U.S.A. and England, which they promulgated among the prisoners there. He, taking advantage of unfavourableness of the news to the Japanese troops, intended to transmit them to Americans and Englishmen intained in the Camp or detained thereabout in order to stir up a feeling of hostility. Conjecturing that the news would be promulgated among the local natives there through Americans and Englishmen, he asked Weynton to give every news and received it.

When he met with Abin and others, he transmitted through them more than ten times in the period from the middle of November 1942 to the end of February 1943, to Mr. Smith, Governor General of former British North Borneo, and other Englishmen detained in Berhala Island at the mouth of the Bay of Sandakan, unfavourable news to the Japanese troops that the severe battle was fought between the Japanese and American fleets with a result of heavy loss on the former side and that the Japanese troops suffered a heavy loss in New Guinea.

He transmitted more than twenty times in the period from December 1942 to July 1943 to Mr. Taylor, a British Doctor, who had

Captain Lionel Matthews G.C., M.C. 8 Div. Signals. Executed 2.3.44
8 Div. Signals Association

been ordered to serve in the Sandakan Citizen Hospital and under surveillance, news unfavourable to the Japanese troops that the U.S. Air Force attacked the Japanese transport ships and sunk 22 warships and ships and brought down many aircrafts in the sea near the Bismark Islands.

He sent to Phillips, an Englishman who was under surveillance in his own house, letters telling the news concerning the situations in the Solomon Sea and New Guinea unfavourable to the Japanese troops several times from May to July 1943.

About May 1943 he intended to construct a radio set to listen to broadcast from America and England and told Weynton and accused Wells his intention and they, in collusion with, asked Abin to get parts of radio set and received them one after another and tried to assemble it secretly under the guidance of Weynton until about June 1943, when they were detected before having finished it.

(ii). Accused Roderick Graham Wells also had a hostile feeling against Japan and had dislike for being a prisoner.

He knew that correspondence and contact with local natives outside the stockade were forbidden for prisoners by order of the Chief of the Camp in about October 1942, but about May 1943 he was told by accused Stevens that Mavar, an Englishman under surveillance, was in the service of the Sandakan Power-Generating-Station as a electric technician, intended to raise Mavar's hostile feeling by secretly transmitting news broadcasted from America and England generally once a week in the period from that time to the middle of June of the same year, and, with continual criminal intent, come into contact with him through Stevens and Chien Pei, and exchanged a letter written in cypher in Roman letters and figures and transmitted about ten times news unfavourable to the Japanese troops that the U.S. Airforce attacked the large group of Japanese transport ships and sunk most of them and shot down many aircrafts.

May 1943 he was invited by Matthews to co-operate in constructing a radio set. From that time to July 1943 he was engaged in assembling secretly the radio set in co-operation with Matthews under the guidance of Weynton.

June 1943 while Weynton was subjected to discipline and detained in the guard room, he listened to the broadcast from America and England with Weynton's radio in place of him and each time he promulgated orally or in writing the news unfavourable to the Japanese troops that ....(they) suffered a heavy loss in Rangoon due to the bombing of the U.S. and British Air Forces and that the

Japanese troops in China were counterattacked by the Chinese troops and were fighting desperately.

(iii). The accused Alfred Stevens had been in the service of the Power-Generating-Station attached to the camp since the end of October 1942, when he was ordered to operate the machines there.

Notwithstanding that the prisoners were forbidden to come into contact or communicate with the natives outside the camp by order of the Chief of the Camp, he, with continual intent, told Wu Kokuang, Chien Pei, etc., Chinese electric workers in the power station, several times during the period from January to July 1943, news unfavourable to the Japanese troops that the U.S. Air Force attacked the large group of the Japanese transport ships and sunk most of them in the sea near the Bismark Islands and so on.

About twenty times during the period from May to July 1943 he sent letters between the accused Wells and Mavar, and several packages containing parts of radio set sent by Mavar to Wells through the accused McMillan, Roffey and Chien Pei. He also acted as intermediary of correspondence and contact between prisoner Matthews and Abin three times in the end of June 1943.

(iv). The accused McMillan and Roffey, the former from about September 1942, and the latter from about February 1943, were engaged in collecting wood from outside the camp and knew that prisoners were forbidden to contact and correspond with natives outside.

McMillan, taking advantage of relaxed watch and with continual criminal intent, twice in the end of May and also in the middle of June 1943, handed to Wells letters and packages sent by Mavar through the accused Stevens and Chien Pei and forwarded to Mavar letters sent by Wells through them.

Roffey, thrice every month during the period from the middle of June to July 1943, received from Wells letters addressed to Mavar and sent them through Stevens and Chien Pei, and received from Stevens letters and packages addressed to Wells by Mavar and handed them to Wells."

Reports indicated Nishihara had gone to Tokyo to discuss with the Advocate General the Matthews' case relative to the Hague Convention. Matthews, the leader of the group, was sentenced to death. Before the decision was handed down, Colonel Suga, the Commander of Prisoner of War and Internee Camps in Borneo, appealed to the Court for lenient sentences and to abide by International Law. He seemed particularly concerned the trial would stand up to International scrutiny.

Captain Matthews was executed by a firing squad of three. Col. Suga then arranged for his burial at the Kuching cemetary. Lt. Col. Walsh, accompanied by Major Johnstone, Lieuts. Ewin and Esler, attended. The service was conducted by a civilian chaplain from the English camp.

Assuming that the statement made by the Chief Judge, Egami Sobei, that the trial was completed by 3 pm, is true, the instructions to prepare the grave were given during the Court proceedings.

Pte. Roy Kent remembers being taken from a working party, with four other men, during the morning, to dig the grave. They later acted as bearers.

That night a piper played "The Lament" in the English camp and was heard throughout the huge compound.

* * * *

Nishihara, having been fully aware of the hopes of the POWs, would now link the two events together. He would have given the PYTHON party the credit for reporting the presence of the Japanese shipping and the losses which followed; he would not have been aware the Allied codebreakers were reading their radio signals and anticipating every movement of their tankers plying the Sibutu Channel to supply their fleet at Tawi Tawi and elsewhere. The War Ministry would have regarded their presence very seriously.

According to Japanese accounts Nishihara spent considerable time talking to the three Australians. Having reached his own conclusion he recommended to General Yamawaki the trial take place. Lt. Col. Maeda, an old soldier of 57 years, was appointed Chief Judge with Lt. Kanazawa, a communications officer of 37 Army H.Q., as junior Judge. Captain Matsumoto, Prosecutor, was assisted by Major Nishihara to question the prisoners. Some reports indicated he was also a Judge.

The trial took place before Christmas 1944 and the men were sentenced to death. Later, Lt. Col. Maeda stated the reasons for condemning the three men: "..... these men were Australian soldiers who had come to Borneo disguised in clothes not an Army uniform. At that time I cannot remember if I had ever seen anyone dressed like the Australian Lieutenant and Sgt.

"The reasons for my condemning the 3 Australians to death were as under:

Lt. General Yamawaki, Commander Japanese 37 Army – Staff Officers with local dignitaries

AWM

(a) the three men said they were soldiers but had entered Borneo in disguise to observe Japanese Army, shipping and natives and to report information on such matters to Australia

(b) they had brought wireless and signal equipment to enable them to transmit information

(c) they had observed Japanese shipping. The Prosecutor, Matsumoto said one of the 3 men had a notebook in which were found entries concerning observation of Jap shipping in Tambisan area

(d) and, as all the above matters contravened Gun Ritsu regulations they were spies and therefore legally deserving of condemning to death. The regulations were South Pacific Army Gun Ritsu.

"These men have committed the acts of spies. Because of the observing and reporting of ship movements Imperial Japanese military operations were affected adversely. This was a breach of an Article of Gun Ritsu therefore they should be executed, because this caused the loss of many of our ships.

"I did not specify the method of execution, and was not present thereat and do not know when it took place."

Lt.Col. Maeda reported to Lt.General Yamawaki the three men were found guilty and he concurred with these findings.

After a few days, the date of carrying out the death sentences was set down for December 30, 1944.

Matsumoto, Prosecutor, said: "The sentence was executed on 30 December 1944. Since I was requested a day or so beforehand by the army stockade to attend this execution, I went to the designated place within the stockade, accompanied by a clerk named Toyama. When we arrived, the defendants had already been placed on the gallows with all the preparations completed. Major Nishihara, the C.O. of the Army Stockade who was in charge of the execution, the Chief Warden, and others were there. The medical officer, 1st Lt. Nagita, too, was there. The regulations did not require the announcement of the method of execution of the military death penalty when the verdict was pronounced. Therefore, the execution officer, according to the Southern Army Military Law had the right to choose the execution method, such as shooting by firing squad or other means.

Since the execution was carried out with no mishap, I returned immediately to my office and therefore do not know anything regarding the burial that followed."

There were many native prisoners in the Batu Tiga Gaol, among them was Sayam and his cousin, Ahong; they had been arrested at Tambisan as suspected of having been involved in assisting the Americans in the Sulus. Sayam remembers the prisoners arriving there: "One of the prisoners was very tall but thin. He was wearing spectacles and was fair haired. The other two were shorter and the shortest had black curly hair. All were dressed in green or khaki colour."

Ahong said: "One day the Kempe Tai took me from my cell together with Sayam and another native to the cell occupied by the Australians. On entering their cell I saw the three Australians standing with their eyes blindfolded and their hands tied behind their backs. The Japanese then ordered us prisoners, in Malay language, to lead the Australians to the gallows. I led one of the shorter men by holding his shoulder and he asked me if the other two Australians were coming to which I replied 'yes'.

"The Japanese Kempe Tai made us lead the Australians up the fifteen stairs of the gallows and stand there on the trap doors. We were then ordered outside." It is now known the three Australians, blindfolded and handcuffed, were brutally battered, fracturing their skulls, prior to the gallows operating. Ahong continues: "After this time I heard the trap doors crash open and the Japanese inside start laughing ....."

* * * *

Japanese officers often said they only recognised International Convention when it was used to their advantage – and this is confirmed by the Prosecutor Matsumoto who stated: "The War Ministry at Tokyo had previously issued an order countermanding some of the provision of the Hague Convention and when I arrived in Borneo I studied the 37 Army order promulgating these variations, the only variation on the Regulations affected the food supply of the prisoners of war; this order was issued by Gen. Lt. Yamawaki – General Officer Commanding 37 Army. He said he knew Japan was a signatory of the Convention and that our Army was obliged to obey its provisions except where otherwise ordered by the War Ministry." The policy of starving the prisoners to render them ineffective in assisting an invasion and ultimately disposing of them was consistent in all forward areas, such directives would have been issued by the War Ministry.

Lt Gen. Yamawaki said: "After one man was apprehended at Tambisan it was established he was an NCO from a Signal unit in Australia. After this the situation became worse. There were reports of white spies penetrating the densely wooded coast between Tambisan Point and Lahat Datu and lights were frequently seen on the sea at night and the situation became uneasy. As the Garrison Unit was extremely small (altogether there were only a thousand men in the north of Borneo) it had no means of transportation other than small vessels.

"By September and October 1944 our forces were greatly reinforced and many changes were made in the disposition of the Garrison troops." These additional troops would have added further demands on the food stocks in Sandakan, thus reducing the POWs food allocation further. Lt.Gen. Yamawaki continues: "While this was going on convincing evidence that the spies who had infiltrated had escaped by sea was found, and the Army gradually recalled the troops who were under the command of Col. Otsuka of the Sandakan Garrison."

The early part of 1944 the strength of the Unit was two companies – the total strength in the whole of Borneo was less than a Division, an ideal situation for guerillas of the Filipino type to further stretch the Japanese defence resources by hit and run tactics. However this type of warfare was not considered at the time, instead, activities were restricted to intelligence gathering.

When the Japanese seized McKenzie and found his note book recording the sighting of ships in the Sibutu Straits, that alone was enough to convince them they were dealing with spies. Much was said about uniforms but it was the knowledge these commandos had reported shipping movements and many of their ships had been lost; from the level of Sandakan intelligence that was sufficient to condemn the men to death. As one of the Judges stated at the trial: "Our ships were sunk by submarines due to the acts of the Defendants, and our Army's strategy had been greatly hindered. In accordance with the Southern Region Administration Regulations the death sentence may be given."

The Japanese were asked why they chose to hang the three Australians instead of carrying out the execution by firing squad as in the Matthews' case. They replied the facility was there, they decided to use it. It would seem they were curious about its function and decided to demonstrate its use. The spontaneous laughter of the 17 Japanese present would indicate it was done partly for entertainment....

Chapter 4

A Section at S.R.D. were given the task of preparing a preliminary plan, code-named Kingfisher. By November 1944 a final submission complete with plans was submitted at Advanced Allied Land H.Q. for consideration.

Basically the report proposed to ascertain what assistance could be given by Services Reconnaissance Department in a combined airborne/naval operation, the object of which was the rescue and evacuation of all prisoners of war from the POW camps in the Sandakan area of British North Borneo. The report then detailed topographical information and the basic knowledge required and the sites of potential dropping zones. The siting of the Sandakan POW Camp made an airborne relief attack and evacuation a feasible operation when it came into range of troop carrying aircraft; dropping zones and evacuation points were available reasonably near the camp; to plan such an attack in the necessary detail required up-to-date intelligence of a very high standard. Detailed intelligence about the routine at the camp would be necessary and essential that the attack be so timed as to find the prisoners con-concentrated there, or, alternatively, their working areas should be very well known. Complete surprise was essential and no time must be allowed between the actual landing and the seizure of the camp area, otherwise the prisoners would be either removed or massacred. The physical condition of the prisoners would make evacuation a big problem. Provision would have to be made in the major plan for POWs unable to walk; this problem would be obviated if the Japanese transport could be located and seized.

The report emphasised the preservation of the security of the main operation was absolutely vital and made it necessary for the reconnaissance party to be inserted by submarine, this method

Sandakan POW Camp and Airfield showing possible Drop Zones.
James M. Kendall. 309 Bombardment Group

being the safest for an initial entry; it was considered that an entry by Catalina was feasible but definitely not so secure, and the type of terrain made it impracticable to drop in a reconnaissance party blind by parachute. Both alternative methods would have required contemporaneous diversionary bombing attacks for them to be feasible.

The timing of the attack would have to take into account the necessity for fighter cover; the north-west monsoon made a landing from a submarine difficult until the end of February or the beginning of March.

The Japanese garrison was both small and dispersed; the scattered nature of the vital points in the area made possible a series of extremely useful diversionary attacks, such as the C.O.'s house, the Governor's house, Post Office for communications, Officers' sleeping quarters etc.

The fact that the prisoners were able to move about outside the camp would make it comparatively easy to contact a senior POW officer who would be able to give much valuable information. Such information could possibly be obtained, with discretion, from local natives who were known to be reliable.

Very little intelligence was available regarding 'E' Force and the 'British POW Camp'. It was absolutely essential that intelligence be obtained of the location and number of POWs (if any) in these two camps; the number of prisoners would make it worthwhile to consider the advisability of dropping arms and equipment into the camp.

The report then further recommended that a reconnaissance party of six, composed of four Europeans and two natives with local knowledge, be inserted by submarine into the Sandakan area as soon as was possible and not less than six weeks before the contemplated operation, and that they be given the task of making a detailed reconnaissance of the area and locate all Japanese ground dispositions and coast defence arrangements, in particular, guards, land and sea patrols, A/A and coast defence sites, radar and land and sea minefields. They would also endeavour to ascertain everything possible about the procedure of the Main POW Camp (and subsidiary if any), the characteristics of the Commander and the routine and layout of the camp or camps. There would be the selection of suitable dropping zones and ascertaining suitable landing beaches for use as evacuation points and routes to same; they would advise on the Japanese communication and alarm systems and the supply of metereorological information if required. All this information was to be relayed to Australia ten days prior to the major operation to allow for detailed planning.

Further tasks for this party during the main operation, the report continued, would be the making of reception arrangements on the dropping zones such as the placing of homing devices, if required, or smoke candles as wind indicators; the dislocation of communications; the provision of guides from dropping zones to objectives and the assistance of the Parachute Battalion to locate transport for conveying POWs to embarkation points. There would also be the provision of guides to these points and the marking of the routes to them.

The report stressed again the need for strict security and stated that the preservation of security was of such paramount importance that it was recommended that all Signals received would be handled by an expert fully familiar with the touch of the transmitting Signallers.

The plan listed all the officers known to be in the Sandakan Camp – set out in unit order. The planners were not to know how the composition of 'B' Force was comprised. Unlike 'A' Force (which departed from Singapore for Burma in 1942) where Brigadier Varley selected his officers to maintain an effective, balanced Brigade group in the event of meeting friendly forces, 'B' Force, under Walsh, was ordered by Changi Command for all Units to provide numbers. Most Units took the opportunity to allocate officers who were surplus to their requirements; many others sent officers who had just arrived in January 1942, only to join their allocated Units as prisoners of war. Normally the Camp Adjutant would have been an officer from one of the established Units. Instead a voyage only officer, Captain Cook, who arrived in January 1942 to be left at G.B.D., took over as Camp Administrator. It appears Hoshijima found him acceptable and kept him in that position. Why Walsh didn't appoint one of his own 2/10 Fld. Artillery to the position is not known – the command at Sandakan was not as strong as it could have been.

The only source of information on 'B' Force came from Wallace, a parade ground NCO, who the planners realised was not well informed enough to advise on matters, and he would not have known of the formation of Captain Mosher's Company to be used for the express purpose of assisting an incoming rescue force. However, the report makes no mention of this vital information – so much Wallace would have not known.

The plan provided to insert a party by submarine and make contact with the POWs. The proposal did not include any provision for, at this early stage, remaining in Sandakan and establishing the airfield to support future operations in North Borneo however it seems G.H.Q. would prefer this option.

In 1944 the planners proposed a rescue operation and not an occupation force. Sandakan was 2000 miles from the nearest major base, Biak, and when Morotai was occupied in September 1944 at some time later it became feasible to commence planning an assault to occupy Sandakan and develop the airfield as part of the OBOE operations.

Prisoners felt they could count on all Australians, that sooner or later they would come. No thought was ever given they were written off or that their mates from the other A.I.F. battalions would not come – they had enlisted together – they were brothers; Australian POWs always dreamed of a bloke rushing in dressed in khaki, not knowing they were now suitably dressed in jungle green, but the dream was there. It was agony to wake up and face the next day, press their fingers into their limbs to determine how the beri beri was worsening – feel their heads for temperature from malaria and inspect the ulcers to see how much pus would have to be removed. Then they would line up, tired, with hunger pains, stiff in the joints, and slump along the Mess line to take the daily issue of sloppy rice or green water – depending on what was available – another day – tonight they will be able to have another dream – it won't be long now –

Intelligence reports clearly indicated the position of a W/T Receiving Station at about the 2 Mile peg, north of the town on the Kabon China Road, guarded by a Japanese outpost of four men. The strength of the detachment was not known. There was a nearby golf course which could provide a possible dropping zone.

The junction of the Kabon China Road and the Sibuga Road, at the 6 Mile peg, was apparently unguarded. There was no alternative road for motor transport from Sandakan Town to the airfield and the POW Camp other than through this road junction.

The POW Camp, about 800 yards north east of the 8 Mile peg and about 300 yards south of the south-west corner of the airfield, contained, in January, 1945, 1,800 A.I.F. prisoners; Intelligence stated it was easy to enter or leave the camp, that dysentery was very bad and that there was a shortage of medicines. The Japanese POW guards numbered forty and were housed nearby in the guardhouse and barracks, south and east of the camp respectively. There was a power station about 400 yards south-west of the camp on the road and a police station at the 8 Mile peg.

The airfield was located about 1600 yards north of the 7 Mile peg on the Kabon China Road. From the 7 Mile peg a road runs north to the airfield, the surface of which is graveled. In February 1944 the dimensions of the airfield were 200 yards by 800 yards. It was proposed to extend it to 1200 yards to the south-east with the runway in a north-south position, to be completed by October of that year. The type and number of aircraft was unknown.

The entrance to the Sibuga River lies about 3,600 yards north of the airfield. This river can be approached from Shallow Bay, and small craft carrying up to 30 men can navigate it at any state of the tide. Approximately 2,500 yards from the mouth of the river on the south bank there is a wharf and a road leading to the airfield.

Potential dropping zones were listed then as the area north- west of Sibuga River; the area immediately west of the airfield and the area of the golf course and north of the W/T Receiving Station.

It was considered that preferably the parties should be inserted by submarine and it was suggested, for consideration by the U.S. Navy, that there was a good dropping point five miles north-east of Bo-Aan Island on the 20 fathom line. From this position the submarine would be approximately 30 miles from Sandakan and screened from possible radar by a group of islets south of Bo-Aan Island.

It was suggested if after discussion with the U.S. Navy that the insertion at that point was impractical during the north-east monsoon, insertion could be by Catalina. Subject to photographic reconnaissance, the following areas would appear possibly to be suitable:

a) The deep water stretches north and south of Pulo Tinbang (Inner Sandakan Harbour).

b) The inner bay area west of Pulo Tinbang, which, though unsurveyed and uncharted, may be considered a feasible landing area on the results of photographic reconnaissance.

c) The deep water channel between Tg, Pandarus (Lat. 6 03'N. Long. 118 E) and Libaran Island.

The map accompanying the early Kingfisher reports did not have the benefit of the air photos taken October 24, 1944, which would have greatly influenced the planners and again, photos taken after the big Liberator raids of December.

Vast areas of forest were cleared by this time by the POW Wood Parties, creating connecting drop zones adjacent to the camp and airfield. If, as had been suggested in November, a reconnaissance had been inserted the rescue plan would have dramatically changed to take the Sandakan area and use it as a Forward Air Base for future operations to be undertaken in British North Borneo and N.E.I.,

At Morotai, Group Capt. Peter Jeffrey, D.S.O., D.F.C., whose brother, Capt. Rod Jeffrey, was a prisoner at Sandakan, asked Air Commodore Scherger why the paratroop battalion was not being brought forward to rescue the prisoners at Sandakan. Scherger replied: "The Unit may be required to be used during the forthcoming Balikpapan invasion." R.A.A.F Historical Section

including Tarakan and Balikpapan.

Since the air attacks commenced in the early months the main defensive line for Sandakan was moved back to Beluran. In the event of an Allied assault the Japs would not have been able to bring up reinforcements quickly – as in other areas, the Japs avoided zones which could be subjected to bombardment.

After Major Steele was de-briefed he was never consulted again on the plan in the belief there could have been a breakdown of security on such a secret proposal.

The matter of evacuation was not addressed – Sandakan was an isolated region with only about 30 miles of road; it relied on sea transport for supplies; there were only about 30 vehicles of all types in the area and most of these were claimed to have been destroyed when the P38s first appeared in September 1944.

The suggestion of diversionary bombing would have alerted the Japanese. Unless the POWs were armed at this time they probably would have been herded into the huts and massacred. The incoming force may have found the Camp officer unprepared for such a rescue operation – Hoshijima may have told him, over the frequent meals they had together, just what they would have done on seeing the suspicious signs of enemy interest; at this time he would have been briefed by the Kempe Tai they had three Australian commandos in the Gaol who had been landed by submarine – their cover story was to assist escaped POWs – accordingly, Hoshijima would have had some plan to prevent a rescue.

It is likely Major Steele would have advised to stay in Sandakan – consolidate, and use the airfield for future operations against other objectives. However, they did not ask Steele – the Americans had to tell S.R.D. what was wrong with the plan.

In January 1945 work ceased at the Sandakan airfield except for small working parties of six men which Hoshijima personally took to the airfield to recover and destroy unexploded bombs. During these visits the POWs observed the ack-ack positions were destroyed – one site of four light ack-ack guns received a direct hit – these results would have been photographed by reconnaissance aircraft. The POWs noted all aircraft destroyed on previous raids were removed and camouflaged in the scrub. The Japanese had no workshop facilities to repair damaged aircraft and maintenance was carried out with men working out on bamboo scaffoldings.

*   *   *   *

The policy of rescuing Allied prisoners of war would have been one for the Allies to determine. There were large concentrations of British and Australians at Singapore, Hong Kong, Kuching and Sandakan; there were Americans at Manila, Cabuatuan, Los Banos, Camp O'Donnell and Davao. Focussing attention in rescuing POWs in one camp located in the regions could have had far reaching repercussions on those under Japanese control. It is most likely Combined Chiefs of Staff decided POWs or Internees would only be relieved in the normal course of military operations.

In the Philippines Fertig was now established in Aguson province, Commander Parsons was anxious to arrange contact with the POW Camp at Davao. Earlier, a number of Americans escaped and made their way north to join the guerillas. One of these men was Colonel Mellnik who was later sent to Washington where he was interviewed by MIS.X., an organisation established to aid POWs and missing airmen. As a result, a plan was developed to investigate what aid could be given to the POWs. Washington approved sending a MIS.X officer, who was then in the South West Pacific, to Mindanao to make contact with the POWs at Davao.

The Philippines Regional Sector of A.I.B. received the plan for execution and objected that the proposal could conflict with Fertig's command. By this long process of getting the matter under way, it was not until 26 April 1944 the matter was approved and Fertig advised:

> "Capt. Harold A. Rosenquist has been placed on temporary duty with your command for the purpose of acting as your adviser in planning of assistance to prisoners of war in your Military area. Such matters will be conducted in accordance with policies of the G.O.C. as communicated to you from time to time."

Later, MacArthur's H.Q. cautioned that the utmost care must be taken in contacting POWs in order to preserve their safety.

Rosenquist's party was landed by submarine in early June 1944 and he made his way with the assistance of guides to Fertig's HQ., Fertig was obviously annoyed that some officer could come into his area on a special mission expecting every assistance from him without disclosing what his mission was. After pressure from Fertig, Rosenquist disclosed that his mission was to free the POWs at Davao POW Camp – and how do you propose moving all the sick? with a hospital ship? Don't you have any idea of the condition of those poor devils?!!" and so the questions flowed as Fertig described the shocking condition the POWs were in and how the Japanese would react – they would massacre those unable to move.

Earlier, the code-breakers picked up the order from Imperial General Headquarters to move the fittest POWs to Japan as shipping became available, all empty ships were to be used. Agents in the Davao area were not to know the cargo on the ships leaving there was human, and most of the POWs were shipped out. The last ship with 750 POWs on board was torpedoed off the west coast of Zamboanga. Like other Japanese orders consistent with Imperial General Headquarters' instructions, Japanese guards were ordered not to allow any POW to escape into Allied hands. Any who were caught were blindfolded and shot; consequently when the torpedo slammed into the ship they opened fire on survivors. Those who swam ashore were assisted by the guerillas. Later, the NARWHAL rescued 83 and took them to Manus for recovery.

The condition of the POWs shocked those who rescued them. At Manus the whole story unfolded of the brutalities the Japs had inflicted on the thousands who died and the knowledge there were still several thousand Americans behind wire was appalling. The Japs demonstrated they would take reprisals against those attempting to escape.

There seems to have been a year lost in organising plans and policies for the relief of POWs in Jap camps. The U.S. were building up a dossier on breaches of the Geneva Convention – they were not to know until 1943 the Japanese did not recognise any Convention but their own and used the sign of the Red Cross for their own purposes. As a result there was so much time lost in producing a policy to relieve the POWs. The U.S. State Department commenced examining ways to assist Allied POWs held by the Japs.

In February 1944 they made a proposal to the Japanese Government, through the Swiss Government, that would allow a ship a safe passage to the southern region to take Red Cross or relief supplies to the prisoner of war compounds at the principal localities. The Japanese accepted this proposal and advised the Swiss Government the name of the ship and the route it would take.

They selected the huge AWA MARU and loaded it with tons of spare aircraft engines and ammunition and just a mere 2000 tons of relief supplies. They broadcast the route she would take. She would go to Singapore and Indonesian ports and return via Hong Kong, Takao, and then through the Formosa Straits to Japan. The ship would bear special markings of a large white cross on each side of the funnels and the white cross would be illuminated at night.

The U.S. submarine Commanders were sceptical about the proposal. The Navy had been suspicious about the large number of hospital ships which had plied the water to and from Japan.

In late 1944 and early 1945 POWs at Singapore were accustomed to loading tin and rubber on to the Hospital ships in Singapore. As the Japanese often stated, they only recognised International Treaties when it suited them. However this proposal, like the proposal to swap Japanese civilians captured in Saipan with American POWs, was a State Department matter and could have some benefit to the POWs. The Allies were never better informed of conditions and locality of POW Camps and the serious conditions of the prisoners and there was genuine concern for their welfare.

The U.S. Navy sent out plain language messages notifying all submarines in detail of the route of the AWA MARU with instructions to let her pass. The vessel was followed south to all loading points where she was loaded with strategic war material and gave her route returning via what the Americans believed to be was a minefield – changing it at the last moment.

The QUEENFISH never got the message straight and mistook the AWA MARU for a destroyer escort; after sinking her the Captain surfaced and sailed through thousands of bales of rubber floating on the surface. He picked up one Japanese survivor who was prepared to be rescued. It was known by now the Japanese used the Red Cross to protect ships carrying war supplies. If they were concerned about the safety of POWs they could have marked ships carrying prisoners and advised the Swiss Government of the name of the ship, the route it was taking and the origin of the prisoners.

The event demonstrated again the frustration the Allies had in endeavouring to do something to assist the POWs.

General Headquarters were obviously concerned and bewildered about how to deal with the recovery of Allied POWs in Japanese hands. Despite this setback plans continued to be made. It was later established that the guerillas, with a little assistance, might have removed most of the men safely had the project been organised when the opportunity presented itself earlier.

The Kingfisher proposal reached Allied Land H.Q. late 1944 where it was closely examined by planners from all Services. At the time the closest airfields were Morotai and Leyte, and both these fields were operating to maximum capacity. The planners decided such an operation would require continuous fighter support and these could not be provided by land bases so far away, therefore, carriers would have to be deployed. At this stage no carriers were operating south of the Philippines as the N.E.I. and Borneo were regarded as having been bypassed and of a lower priority.

Despite this aspect, the examination continued until a large amphibious Task Force with many escorts and support vessels emerged. It was assumed the Japanese would have mined the waters off Sandakan – thus, mine sweepers would be required – hospital ships – with landing barges to move the sick and a tank landing ship to provide transport and infantry to support the paratroops. The planners decided Kingfisher was impractical at the time as it would delay operations in the Philippines for two months This was unacceptable and, accordingly, it was abandoned. Despite this, they agreed Sandakan would be relieved in the normal course of on-going military operations, the plan for which was now nearing finality. It was well down the list of priorities. The Intelligence parties now being prepared to be inserted – representing the early phase of Kingfisher – would continue; however, the Kingfisher proposal was abandoned.

MacArthur's plans for the re-occupation of British North Borneo and the East Indies called for a campaign which would commence with the seizure of Japanese held oil resources in British North Borneo as soon as land based air support could be made available within the range of the objective. The VICTOR 4 operations being the seizure of Palawan and the Sulus were ideally suited for the occupation of British North Borneo. The Americans had learnt that any campaign acquiring airfields it was important they be seized prior to the wet season in order that airfield construction was not hampered.

On February 3, 1945, General MacArthur informed Washington of the proposed operations against British North Borneo and the Netherlands East Indies to secure the oil fields which might be required to supplement supplies for the drive against the Japanese homeland.

He requested shipping to move the 1 Aust. Corp of two Divisions which were then located in Queensland and New Guinea. He also advised the plans were under way to establish air power at Puerto Princessa, Palawan, Zamboanga and Sulu to support the amphibious operations into North Borneo.

On the same day, General Berryman, Chief of Staff Allied Land Headquarters wrote to General Sir Thomas Blamey, C.in.C. of Australian Military Forces, advising him of the draft schedule of operations commencing February 25 to secure Puerto Princessa and on March 8, Zamboanga. The 9 Division would probably be used to secure Jesselton-Brunei Bay and Miri oilfields and later carry out operations against Sandakan, if Australian POWs were still there, by using the 1 Aust. Parachute Battalion if aircraft were available. Later Tarakan would be secured by Australian 7 Division.

As the first death march got under way from Sandakan 29 January 1945 MacArthur's armoured columns moved into Manila. Their immediate mission was to free the civilian internees at Santo Tomas University. Upon their arrival the advance elements broke through the gates of the campus wall. Inside, the Japanese Army guards – mostly Formosans – put up little fight and within a few minutes some 3,500 internees were liberated amid scenes of pathos and joy none of the participating American troops will ever forget. In another building away from the main quarters, some sixty Japanese under Lt.Col. Hayashi, the Camp Commandant, held as hostages another 275 internees, mostly women and children. Hayashi demanded a safe conduct from the ground for himself and his men before he would release these internees. General Chave, the

Division Commander, had to accept the Japanese conditions; Hayashi and his men left next morning.

While the release was under way and the landing units pushed further on, they came across the old Bilibid Prison, which seemed deserted. During this period there was confusion and troops came upon heavy fire from the nearby Far Eastern University. At one stage it was believed if the Japanese had counter-attacked they would have had to abandon the internees at Santo Tomas. Next day Infantry broke into the Bilibid Prison and discovered approximately 800 Allied and American prisoners of war and 530 civilian internees.

General Chave said they had no idea prisoners of war and internees were held there. On 5 February the 37 Division removed both prisoners and internees when fire threatened the area and it appeared the Japanese were preparing for a counter-attack. The prisoners and internees departed so hurriedly they had to leave their pitiful belongings behind; when they returned a few days later the looters had stolen almost everything.

After MacArthur was celebrating the occupation of Manila on February 6, he gave orders for the capture of Palawan and other objectives in the Sulu Archipelago.

MacArthur wanted to be certain he had the situation on Luzon well under control before he committed elements of the Eighth Army to objectives in the southern Philippines. While he was prepared to leave large numbers of Japanese isolated in the Solomons-New Guinea area he felt a moral obligation to occupy the whole of the Philippines because he promised them he would return. This promise was stamped on every shipment to the guerillas who passed evidence of MacArthur's plan to every village in the country. This program did not clash with other operations in the central Pacific and there was adequate shipping available in the region at the time. These operations would be self supportive on land based air support and all objectives would have airfields for development for future operations. General Eichelberger, Commander of the 8th Army, had four Divisions available to him, in addition he had at his disposal the 503 Parachute Rgt. As the VICTOR operation was planned early in the year it was obvious it was in preparation for the occupation of North Borneo and very much part of the original OBOE I – Jesselton – Brunei Bay – Miri – Seria oilfields.

The Palawan landing took place on February 28 and the airfield was operational by March 10; losses – 10 killed. Zamboanga was taken on March 10 – an airfield with a 5000 ft. runway was constructed and in operation by March 15. The next objective was

Sanga Sanga, a small island on the western tip of Tawi Tawi – the strip was extended to 5000 feet and by May 2 fighters of the 13th Airforce had moved in. Just 40 miles from British North Borneo. Tawi Tawi represented the boundary of the Demarcation Line between the Philippines and Borneo. There appears to have been British resentment allowing the U.S. to become involved in what was a British Colony on one hand and American disinterest in assisting Britain re-establish a control of the colony. One would have thought some representation would have been made after the Kingfisher project was abandoned to examine the possibility of seizing Sandakan as part of the VICTOR operation.

Closer co-operation and liaison with the Americans could have convinced them to include the seizure of Sandakan with the VICTOR operations – thus acquiring an airfield suitable for heavy aircraft on the mainland of Borneo to give close support for future operations against Brunei and Sarawak. The Japanese may not have reacted violently towards the POWs under their control at such an orderly operation – whereas with a specially planned operation to release the POWs they were more likely to take repercussions against other concentrations.

When Jesselton-Brunei Bay-Miri were designated OBOE 1 it was planned as an advanced base for 1 Aust. Corp of two Divisions and possibly three, together with supporting Airforce and Naval units. The U.S. had suggested Brunei Bay be developed as a major British Naval Base for their Pacific Fleet – the British declined and said they would have Singapore before the Brunei Bay base could be constructed and completed. MacArthur proposed the N.E.I. and British North Borneo area of command be transferred to S.E.A.C. July 1. The U.S. regarded this area as British responsibility. Later the date was put forward until after the capture of Singapore.

General Headquarters had indicated early in February there could be changes, and these came about in late February. OBOE 1 Jesselton was to become Tarakan. This was brought about because planners sought an airfield located geographically to service both North Borneo and Balikpapan. Tarakan was the logical site if the intelligence the Dutch provided proved to be reliable.

At the same time, a reassessment of the Jesselton-Labuan airfields favoured Labuan as the Japanese had constructed two airfields there. In addition, the island was lightly defended and effectively controlled Brunei Bay, the most important strategically placed base in North Borneo. One of the airfields on Labuan was constructed by 300 POWs under the command of Captain Hirowa Nagai, formerly Hoshijima's Adjutant at the Sandakan Camp. Most of them died there, and the remainder were moved to Riam Road where the survivors were massacred. Nagai was then moved to Paginatan where he supervised the torturous rice carrying parties.

With the changes Tarakan was the next objective with a target date of 29 April, later to become May 1. In addition, the PETER operations were replaced by OBOE objectives.

The program now was Tarakan – May 1, Labuan, Miri – June 10, Balikpapan – July 1. Early in February the Americans, at the Yalta Conference, informed the British they would not be able to provide American troops for the conquest of the N.E.I. The original concept of planning up to February was that an assault would take place against Jesselton on April 1. At that time during April there would have been 1000 POWs at Sandakan, just a couple of hundred miles away. This change to Tarakan was to contribute largely to the fate of those remaining at Sandakan.

For several months there was much discussion at G.H.Q. on the future objectives; at this time changes in Allied Intelligence Bureau had given rise to the ascendence of a Dutch officer, Colonel S.H. Spoor, who later became Director of the N.E.I. Sub-Section and sought direct contact and liaison with G2. G.H.Q. Colonel Spoor was the senior Dutch Army Intelligence Officer in Australia, responsible directly to Lieut. General Van Ouyen, C.in.C. R.N.I.A. He also sought, and gained, direct access to General Blamey's H.Q., however, that would be terminated later.

Senior Australian officers at Advanced Allied Land Headquarters at Morotai were aware of the intense lobbying taking place by Col. Spoor pushing hard for the 1 Australian Corps to be used for the recapture of the Netherlands East Indies. Spoor realised if the Australians were successful in persuading MacArthur to accept their participation in the main drive to Singapore or towards Japan the N.E.I. occupation would have to wait. The Dutch urgently needed the oil to generate income – at this time the war in Europe was nearing its end. MacArthur had not met the resistance he expected, otherwise he may have used the 6 Australian Division to land at Aparri in the north of Luzon.

*   *   *   *

The Joint Chiefs of Staff, now with the knowledge of Japanese intentions to kill the remaining POWs and Internees, instructed MacArthur to plan and rescue the last remaining concentration of internees held at Los Banos Agricultural College in Southern Luzon.

The official U.S. Air Force History stated: "...... in a carefully planned and skilfully executed amphibious and paratroop raid, elements of the 11th Airborne Division on 23 February 1945 had liberated 2,147 internees at Los Banos Agricultural College near the southern shore of Laguna de Bay. The airborne phase of the raid, flown by ten C47s of the 65th Troop Carrier Squadron with 125 paratroopers from Nichols Field, was precisely coordinated with the arrival of infiltration parties; at 0700 the paratroopers dropped at the edge of the college grounds and joined infiltrators to surprise the Japanese guards at physical training before they could reach their weapon racks. Co-operating fighters strafed and bombed parties of Japanese in the vicinity. Such was the complete surprise that only two Americans were killed as compared with 243 Japanese."

In addition to the Army Airforce statement the Army Historian gave more detail of the operation: "a task force composed of the 1st Battalion, 188th Glider Infantry, elements of the 511th Parachute Infantry, attached guerillas and supporting artillery, tank destroyers, and amphibious tractors made a daring, carefully timed rescue of 2,147 internees from an internment camp near Los Banos on Laguna de Bay. Guerillas and elements of the 188th Glider Infantry invested the camp by land, coming in from the west; other troops of the 188th Infantry came across Laguna de Bay by amphibious tractors, and 'troopers of the 511th Infantry dropped onto the camp proper.

"Annihilating the Japanese garrison of nearly 250, the task force escaped through enemy controlled territory before Fujishige was able to organise a counterstroke."

It now appears that details of the Los Banos operation were not made public for fear of repercussions elsewhere; certainly Australian officers at Advanced H.Q. had no knowledge of the operation otherwise the matter of the plight of those at Sandakan would have been raised. Notwithstanding, it is believed no specific action to recover the POWs would have taken place, any action would have given the Japanese the opportunity to remove all the Military personnel from the Kuching Compound and march them off down the road to their death.

Bessie Sneed, in her book, "Captured by the Japanese", was an internee at Los Banos in February 1945. She wrote: "Early one morning I heard planes of a different sound and got out of the barracks just in time to see transports flying fairly low over the centre of the camp. My husband, who saw the same aircraft from the door of his barracks, came over to me as fast as his strength would permit. The skies were filled with paratroopers. It was the happiest day of our lives.

"The majority of the paratroopers landed close to the barracks housing the Japs, the operation was beautifully timed, catching most of the Japanese out doing sitting up exercises and many of them were killed before they could reach for their arms.

"The Philippino Guerillas who aided in our rescue came through the fence at the end of the Compound, surprising and killing all the Jap guards on duty in that area."

MacArthur's H.Q. were well informed of the condition of the internees – most were mobile and able to move around the camp freely.

At this time the starvation program set in motion in early 1944 had taken effect. Marshal Teruchi, Commander in Chief of the Southern Region, had decided in December the main Allied threat would come on the west coast in the Brunei Bay area and accordingly he ordered General Baba, who took up command of the 37 Army in December, to move eight of his ten Battalions to the west coast. Captain Yamamoto, C.O. of the 2nd Battalion, 25 Regt., who came from Manchuria in October, had moved the first batch of POWs to Ranau and other troops from the airfield locality had also moved west. Sandakan was now lightly held and despite the condition of the POWs there were many able to assist an assault force.

In camp the routine was regular. There were four guard points around the perimeter; the total number of guards responsible for POW control was approximately forty. They were housed in the Jap barracks; the officers, apart from Hoshijima the Camp Commandant who lived at Wong's house, were in an adjacent building.

Each morning, at 7 a.m., the guards would be called out, unarmed, shirts off, and put through physical exercise for some twenty minutes. At this time there were four guards on duty. The maximum firepower available to them – four MGs and no more than ten .303 rounds – was in the guard hut; some believed they were issued with five rounds per guard, however it was known no extra ammunition was carried apart from that contained in the magazine.

The guards on the perimeter were not connected by telephone. They were exposed and could be observed quite clearly. At this critical time all the POWs were concentrated in the camp; no guards would have been in the POW huts. The nearest Japanese troops were at the airfield 1½ to 2 miles away, where there were approximately thirty; other groups were located at points from the 11 Mile to the 16 Mile peg where the few remaining vehicles and fuel was located.

Towards Sandakan there was the W/T Station and about 200 troops scattered and well dispersed in the general area of the golf course.

There were no serviceable Jap aircraft at the airfield. About this time the Japs were so used to seeing Allied planes they did not expect any of their own and when one did show up unexpectedly it was shot at by L.M.G. fire and every Jap present fired up at it with his rifle.

At other Jap barracks or concentrations in the area their soldiers would most probably be going through the same routine. At Hoshijima's house there would be his batman and some house assistants, possibly native helpers. In earlier times he liked to show off with his POW chauffeur, Clarrie Grinter, Hoshijima supplied him with a uniform of a sort, however this softer life possibly affected his chances of surviving on the first march. When Hoshijima ran out of petrol Grinter lost his job.

The night before the proposed assault, arms for POWs would have been delivered to a position outside the camp perimeter for them to recover during the night. Out along the road to Ranau ambushes would have been set up in readiness. The cooks would have been up early preparing the morning meal. From all appearances to the Japs it was just another day, then, in minutes, on the signal, the guards would have been wiped out, fighters would have swooped in attacking the W/T Post at Sandakan and all known concentrations and movement along the entire sixteen miles of road. Paratroop drops would have now commenced, while POWs and sick would have been warned to remain in a calm position and the those able and willing would have been armed.

Since their arrival in Borneo, selected platoons were nominated as a fighting force within the POW Camp. After September 1943 when the officers were taken away these groups continued to be recognised and were always alert to the possibility of taking the camp over as sometimes there were as few as 20 guards present, however the average was about 40. They had plans to rush the guards, disarm them and not only hold the camp but also the airfield for fortyeight hours. They knew the locality of the machine guns and were very confident that with the arms they had buried they could do their part.

As the first Allied aircraft appeared over the camp in September 1944 optimism grew, and so did the plans take shape as to what action the POWs would take; there were many outstanding senior NCOs fully aware of the possibilities that may occur once the Allied forces got close to the area.

There were three recognised exits on the camp perimeter; prior to the POWs going out they would arrange with a mate to keep watch during their absence. When the returning POW approached the exit he would throw a stone towards his mate. If all clear, a stone would be thrown back – this was almost a nightly practice. It would have been comparatively easy to get a few commandos into the camp.

When John Orr was shot at close range on a dark night near the exit by the Jap guard the general belief in the camp at that time was the Japs had been informed by someone friendly to them of the locality where men went through the wire. From my own personal knowledge, the Japanese avoided going out on a black night alone.

It was during this period Owen Campbell met the mystery figure on the Wood Cutting party who never returned but built up the hope that they were not forgotten.

On May 20, 1945, the leader of the AGAS Intelligence party operating north of Sandakan was extracted by flying boat and taken to Morotai. During his de-briefing he mistakenly informed A.I.B. all the prisoners had been moved from Sandakan.

On May 27, aircraft from 13th Airforce and American PT boats together with 13 Kittyhawks of 76 Squadron R.A.A.F., carried out an attack on Sandakan. During this attack, Australian POWs were strafed and a number killed. This attack caused the Japs to panic and commence the second march and the ultimate murder of those 288 men left behind. It was during this strafing one man, in desperation, raced out of the hut holding an Australian flag and waved it frantically, but the raid continued. Later his mates asked him where he got the flag from – he had concealed it in his gear since the fall of Singapore.

General Baba later stated: "I received a telegram from the Sandakan Garrison on the morning of May 27 informing him Allied Naval forces in co-operation with the Airforce launched an attack against Sandakan from dawn on the same day and severe fighting was going on at the moment and five or six warships invaded into the Bay and were shelling by ship guns. But the communication was suspended by noon and we could not communicate with them for the ensuing ten days and there-about. On or about 10 June the communication was re-established and we came to know what had occurred at Sandakan."

It seems that A.I.B. in Morotai was convinced Chester's information given on his de-briefing on May 20 was reliable and accurate; however, other messages to Harlem and Sutcliffe in the field requesting confirmation of Chester's fateful advice seems to indicate some doubt.

Captain Takakuwa burned the POW huts and herded the sick out into the open, the rest of the POWs commenced their march to Ranau.

Dick Braithwaite described the start of the second march:

"When we moved out of the camp they set fire to it; we knew that was pretty final as far as we were concerned. There were about 150 hospital patients just about on their last legs, we were all out in this open field and a Catalina came over with a fellow standing in the doorway looking down at us and I felt if I could jump a bit higher he could grab my hand and take me with him! They didn't do anything, just flew over at very low altitude and had a look.

"We had to leave most of our things we'd made behind. I'd made a chess set out of black hard ebony and bulloak but I couldn't carry it; blokes had hacked guitars out of solid bits of timber, it was like losing home seeing those things go up in smoke, we watched it all go up in flames and we thought "well, we've got nothing".

"It was evening when our march started, I said goodbye to Jimmy Thompson and a few others, hoping to see them along with the fellows who were lying on the ground at the new camp, and we marched off along the bitumen road as far as it went. It was dark, we passed a few small huts along the way, occasionally we would hear a bit of a scuffle followed by a shot and you'd realise someone had tried to make a break for it in the dark; I wondered how many had made it and how they would get on with the locals because we didn't know what the situation was there.

"We marched to the 15 Mile peg at the end of the road and were issued with a bucket of rice to each party of 50. We marched all night along the track, sometimes it was moonlight, sometimes it was showers, you could just see the shadow of the person in front of you; we were kept going until 2 o'clock the next day when we were allowed to have a rest near a small spring. It was now raining very heavily, we washed out our muddy clothing and tried to rest. Then we got an air raid, I don't know whether they could see us or not but here was a bit of activity somewhere because they strafed the area and quite a few took off there; I didn't think about it there for it was too close to the area where we didn't know what the situation was, the people may not have been friendly and would have reported you."

In the meantime, heavy fighting continued at Tarakan.

Chapter 5

General Headquarters (G.H.Q.) received and relied on the information supplied to them by Colonel S.H. Spoor of the Netherlands East Indies Intelligence Service.

The NEFIS report on the airfield on Tarakan stated it possessed hard-stands for 150 bombers and 150 fighters, revettments for 5 bombers and 5 fighters – its elevation was 10-20 feet above sea level and one report said it was not used by the Japanese because they did not possess aircraft.

A.I.B. and officers of Military Intelligence questioned the conflicting accounts coming in relating to the airfield. Two different reports stated the airfield's elevation was from 3 ft. to 10 ft. and from 10 ft. to 20·ft. above sea level. Air photographs supported the lower level, these contradictions placed a doubt on information supplied from N.E.I. sources. The problem was the misinformation, supplied by Col. Spoor was accepted by, and was now appearing as, G.H.Q. intelligence after being processed which gave it authenticity. However Australian Intelligence staff challenged Col. Spoor to provide hard evidence on the availability of stone, coral and material suitable for airfield construction. At this time he produced pictures of quarries, quarry equipment alleged to have been located on Tarakan.

MacArthur's G.H.Q. issued a Handbook intended as a guide for the use of officers in the forward area. On the subject of resources and construction material, "Gravel was obtained from S. Bengawan and POSSIBLY from the hills. Pebbles and boulders (to be broken and used for surfacing) were obtained from the mainland, probably near S. Sekata. Coral was brought by the natives in prahus from the neighbourhood (locality unknown)." A geological map was also provided which showed the bulk of the island comprised unconsolidated clay and some sands and younger sediments, soft, well-bedded shale and minor sandstones. No igneous rocks present. It is surprising the planners did not take note of this vital information produced by G.H.Q. Obviously at this time they were assured there was ample construction material available for roads and airfield construction. The Dutch imported material from the mainland to construct the airfield at Tarakan and when the airstrip was extended by the Japanese, they also brought stone from the same source.

During April three large, four engined bombers were seen at the end of the airstrip on Morotai. No one had seen this type of aircraft before; they were the Photo Reconnaissance B29s, known as the F13, specially fitted out with banks of cameras specifically designed for photographing large areas and now on a special mission to survey major targets in the N.E.I.

The 13th A.A.F. photographed all local airfields within staging range of the Philippines in September/October 1944 in preparation for destroying or rendering them unserviceable, thus preventing the Japanese from reinforcing their airforce defending the Philippines. Intelligence operations received the information supplied by the Dutch and felt it was not adding up – consequently the capability of the airfield was downgraded. Planners believed it could service the 1st Tactical Airforce.

On March 20, 1945, there was a further set back for those left at Sandakan; following a Conference at G.H.Q. to discuss the OBOE II Balikpapan operations one of the decisions reached was: "Owing to limited air facilities at Tarakan employment of 1 Aust.Para.Bn. is undesirable from the A.A.F. view point. It should only be used if its tactical importance is such as to take priority over air support of the operation."

It was obvious Australian officers were anxious to bring the Battalion forward at this time, however, since the down-grading of the airfield it was restricted hopefully to Fighter Squadrons. Command adopted a 'wait-and-see' attitude. Palawan would have been a suitable alternative where R.A.A.F. 81 Wing was based.

Australian Intelligence still required up-to-date material and arranged for an S.R.D. party, code-named SQUIRREL, to be inserted into the area. This party, under Captain Prentice, was inserted by Catalina. Later several natives were `hijacked' from their fishing boats and taken to Morotai for interrogation, there was no brief to check the state of the airfield or to collect soil samples.

From March, units of 1 Aust. Corps commenced landing on

Morotai in preparation for OBOE 1 operations against Tarakan. The A.I.F. would be supported by the R.A.A.F. Operational Command, known as the 1st Tactical Airforce.

When MacArthur informed General Morshead the 26 Bde. would be used to take Tarakan he selected a fine Brigade with a distinguished Commander – Brigadier D.A. Whitehead, C.B.E., D.S.O., M.C., Mentioned in Despatches. Whitehead graduated at Duntroon in 1916 and later served in France. At the outbreak of World War 11 he was promoted Lt. Colonel to command. He trained and took the 2/2 MG Bn. to the Middle East. It was not long before he was transferred to command the 2/32 Battalion at Alamein and later promoted Brigadier in command of the 26 Bde., which distinguished itself there.

After the 9 Division returned to Australia it was involved in the New Guinea Campaign September 1943 – January 1944 on the Huon Peninsula; now highly trained in jungle warfare and amphibious operations it was to embark on its second major campaign in the S.W.P.A. When Whitehead received the order to take Tarakan he set about obtaining fresh intelligence. He later recorded: "We got the usual mass of information – geographic handbooks, engineer surveys, and Dutch reports from people who were here before the war, and based on these certain ideas became fixed.

"We immediately found however a number of discrepancies and contradictions. For example the mud at the beaches; reports varied from the statement that the mud was up to one's armpits at ten yards from the shoreline, to the statement that a ten ton Dutch tank could drive along the beach at low tide. So we had to scrap most of this information and start from the beginning. We were immediately up against the difficulty of getting the aerial photographs we required. Photographs were required to be taken at high and low and medium tides to establish the grade and composition of the beaches. We got a stray oblique photograph and found that the underwater obstacles were quite formidable. We howled for aerial photographs and also got hold of Captain Whitehead (ex-Professor of Geology at Brisbane University) and went into every detail possible.

"We also got two Dutch officers who had been on the island and who had helped in the construction of the underwater obstacles. They were able to advise how far the obstacles were sunk in the mud, when they were erected and how they were driven in. We then had coloured photographs taken and by parallax system were able to measure the depth of the water. The underwater obstacles were all of Dutch construction. One difficulty was in deciding in what condition they were.

"The anti-tank ditch on the west side of the road to the airfield had us worried. It was divided into sections with streams coming through. S.R.D. contacted a native who said he knew another native who had been in Tarakan recently, so the Catalina set off and collected this man. As a result it was decided it was a fire ditch as well. The whole of this defence had been constructed by the Japs. We asked for low obliques and these showed tanks fitted to run oil into the ditch. We were puzzled because of their position which was bordering the swamp. It was decided that the Japs, with inadequate operation reports, thought the Alligators would cross the swamp. From an anti-tank point of view the ditch was a complete waste of labour as the swamp was impassable to the Alligators.

"From the information obtained from the low obliques we made a complete revision and produced our own summaries, gradients of the beach and mud curves. We got the Air Force to do over and actually bomb the mud itself to see whether the craters filled in. On this we planned the assault and type of landing craft to be used, the part of the beach to be used."

Arrangements were now being made to allocate R.A.A.F. to go forward with the assault force; Whitehead was greatly concerned he would be unable to provide sufficient transport for R.A.A.F. requirements and requested they revise the number of vehicles to be taken forward to be used on this small island. The R.A.A.F. Liaison Officer, Wing Commander Ranger, reported to an Inquiry, in May 1945, that the R.A.A.F. were not being honest in their claim for shipping, he stated in his view the A.I.F. had been open and sincere in stating the exact position at any time to the R.A.A.F. and that the R.A.A.F. had made statements which could not be proved. The statement that all vehicles allowed to be transported in the assault shipping were essential for the functioning of the Unit was incorrect. Wing Cdr. Ranger further reported for example the Senior Equipment Staff Officers had assured the Planning Representative for No.78 Wing the vehicles were absolutely essential, yet, reported the Wing Commander, the Commanding Officer of No.78 Wing had assured him that his Wing could carry out their commitments in OBOE I with 48 vehicles less. This was only one example of false information being given to 1st Australian Corps by the R.A.A.F.

Lack of shipping in OBOE 1 made a cut in total logistic imperative. While Ranger endeavoured to see Whitehead's problem of shipping space other officers in 1st Tactical Airforce were not prepared to co-operate and criticised Ranger for being 'too close to the A.I.F.' "I was told that they suspected I had changed my boots from black to brown and that it was a bad thing for me to have been posted close to the Army because I had got too sympathetic towards them, and I was removed forthwith from my position and posted to 77 Wing. To amplify my statement about wearing of tan boots, I would like to add the officer who took my place, Wing Cdr. Honey, was forbidden living with the Army. Furthermore he was told to operate from his H.Q. and only to go down there and see them occasionally", reported Wing Commander Ranger.

The total strength of the R.A.A.F. T.A.F. had grown to 17,000 and as the build-up continued there was reported a surplus of personnel on Morotai, reminiscent of the verse:

"There were Wing Commanders
And Squadron Leaders
And Group Captains too –
Hands in their pockets and
Nothing to do!"

While R.A.A.F. Command was able to find transport to expand their ground staff for future operations despite the fact pilots were complaining of the lack of targets and activity, no transport could be provided to bring the 1st Australian Paratroop Battalion forward to Morotai.

Fed up with the general situation in the area and lack of activity, several officers lodged their applications to resign their commissions on 30 April 1945. At this time the 1st T.A.F. came under R.A.A.F. Command. Air Commodore Cobby consulted Air Vice Marshal Bostock, who interviewed seven of the eight applicants at Air Commodore Cobby's office. Bostock was unsuccessful in establishing the reasons leading up to the resignations, except Group Captain Arthur said they had lost confidence in the R.A.A.F. generally and the way the war was being prosecuted. Bostock sought the officers to withdraw their applications and tear them up — he suggested the word 'forthwith' in the applications indicated their desire to avoid the OBOE operations. Group Capt. Arthur indicated that was not their intention – the word 'forthwith' was changed to 'at the end of current operations'. The pilots did not want to be left behind in a secondary role, many had fought from Europe through the Middle East and were looking forward to being in the forefront of operations against the Japanese homeland.

Bostock sent off a message to Air Vice Marshal Jones, Chief of Air Staff, reporting the problem of command and recommended that Air Commodore Cobby, Group Capt. Simms and Group Capt. Gibson be transferred. The message detailed the circumstances and he showed Cobby the message before despatching it. He also recommended Scherger be appointed to replace Cobby. Air Vice Marshal Jones promptly got himself to Morotai. As it happened, General George

Kenny, Allied Air Force Commander, was there conferring with General Morshead and Air Vice Marshal Bostock on the subject of air support for the Tarakan operation which, in the early stages, would involve the 13th U.S. Airforce. Kenny heard of the problem with the officers and, according to Air Vice Marshal Jones in his book, "From Private to Air Marshal", said, "I demand to see the Officers concerned", and immediately Jones replied, "I must point out that the matters under Enquiry are purely disciplinary ones, they are therefore completely outside your jurisdiction. However, as a matter of co-operation between our two Forces and since you've come all the way from the Philippines, I'll parade the Officers for you."

Kenny urged the officers not to 'hand in their badges' and pointed out in times of war there were always times when Units would have to play a less aggressive role. During the interview, General Kenny said, "Now you have just a small bunch of chaps here. Does this thing go any further than merely yourselves?" The reply given to him was, "Yes, it does. Our views are shared by at least 80% of pilots in the R.A.A.F.", said one of the officers present. Jones said, "I could see Kenny was becoming more and more angry during the course of the interview and by the time it was finished he was seething with fury. As soon as the officers had left he turned on me, "You had to stay and listen to everything I had to say – evidently you don't trust me!"." Jones repeated it was a disciplinary matter and wholly his concern, and he continues in his book, "Kenny was so angry I expected him to physically attack me, I was ready for him." This statement demonstrated again the conflict in the Administration of the R.A.A.F. – which the Government failed to remedy.

Jones returned to Melbourne and went to the Minister for Air, Arthur Drakeford, and requested he appoint a Commissioner to inquire into the matters of the officers requesting to resign their commissions, and also the matter of trading in alcohol.

One would have thought these matters would have been dealt with under existing Regulations by the R.A.A.F – that was not to be.

J.V. Barry, K.C. was appointed Commissioner on 11 May 1945. In the meantime, the war continued, the turmoil in the R.A.A.F and the death rate at Sandakan –

Following, Scherger's appointment as A.O.C. 1st Tactical Airforce, Wing Commander Ranger was back on the job, only to discover the feasibility of establishing an air operational base at Tarakan had not been fully addressed. Officers were now concerned, after studying the air photographs of the airstrip, that it was water-logged. One senior officer borrowed a Mitchell bomber and made a low level inspection of the airstrip, reporting it was doubtful if it was

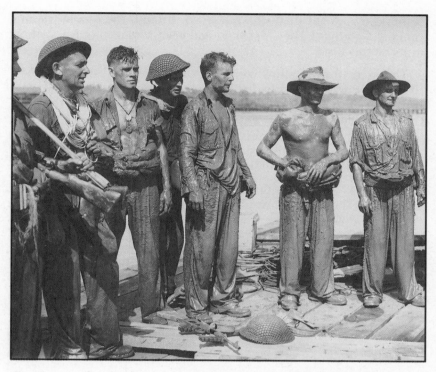

Engineers after having cleared the underwater obstacles. AWM.90915

repairable. He was told, 'Orders were orders'.

Blamey was at Morotai to see the 26 Bde. on its way, it so happened it was Anzac Day 1945 – this must have brought a lot of memories to the men already aboard the convoy and many of these soldiers would have been attending school when the 8 Division first went to Malaya in 1941. Blamey moved along and inspected the troopships from a Naval pinnace.

A few days earlier, Captain 'Jock' McLaren of the 8th Division who escaped from Berhala Is. near Sandakan Harbour and remained fighting the Japanese in the Philippines, was taken by submarine from Morotai to inspect the underwater defences of Lingkas; he spent the night feeling his way along the defences and at daybreak the submarine rendezvoused and took him back to Morotai to report to Brigadier Wills, Controller of A.I.B. The up-to-date information was quickly conveyed to the engineers whose duty it was to blast the breaks in the defences to allow the assault forces to pass through.

The Brigade group arrived off Tarakan at 0400 – it was going to be a long day – at dawn many thought of the landings in the campaign but they also thought of Gallipoli; at this landing all ranks comprised younger men who had been through the jungle training camp at Canungra, the older men had been screened out of combat units by this time.

The escorting warships commenced the bombardment at 0640, this havoc continued while the Engineers went in to blast 60 ft. gaps in the beach defences to enable the Infantry to land. Further out, the Infantry battalions were unloading from the MANOORA, WESTRALIA and un-named L.C.Ts. The 2/48 Bn., already on deck at dawn, watched the bombardment but were particularly impressed with the rocket ships pounding target areas.

There was apprehension amongst the officers and troops going ashore that the Japanese would flood strategic areas with oil and fire it, which would engulf the troops. The B24s had given the oil tanks a good going over despite the order from G.H.Q. not to destroy oil facilities unless it was absolutely necessary. The wording of this order seemed to be to placate the Dutch who did not want the oil facilities destroyed. The Dutch recommended the refinery to be taken by paratroops in order to capture it in working order. It was during the attack on Singapore the Japanese were concerned the

Troops going ashore Tarakan   AWM.90812

British would fire the Straits of Johore to prevent a Japanese landing. Assaulting while Japanese held oil installations and ports was a real danger while stocks of oil were present.

Tarakan, with its soil composition and forest, made it ideal to prepare tunnels and defensive positions – these normally were of a standard design linking a complex system together beneath a hill top. With ample timber these positions could be difficult to overcome.

The troops were told the campaign would only last ten days and after a rest they would probably head for North Borneo and rejoin the Division and possibly be involved in the recapture of Sandakan. Landing Battalions were being attacked by Jap machine-guns from the shore because the R.A.A.F. were running late with the smokescreen they were to lay, however full support from the landing craft soon silenced the enemy fire. The Engineers carried out their formidable task with absolute efficiency and by midday most of the obstacles, which were originally placed there by the Dutch, were blasted.

Famous Battalions of the Brigade were soon ashore leaving Japanese dead on their trail. The scene was one of desolation with little cover for the enemy to interfere with the assault troops. Soon after the 2/24 was landed and followed through the 2/48 to prepare for their positions for the ultimate attack on the airfield. The 2/23, after landing, moved towards Tarakan Hill. By nightfall, the Brigade held an area 2,800 yards wide at the base and up to 2,000 yards in depth. On the left the objectives had been reached, but to the east, Milko, which was among the objectives, was still in the hands of the enemy.

The rear areas were still under fire from snipers. In the afternoon of the 1st, a patrol of the 2/3rd Pioneer Battalion, the principal Unit of the beach group, clashed with parties of Japanese near Burke Highway, and during the first night snipers or shell fire wounded six members of the battalion.

Meanwhile the beach had been a scene of strenuous and often frustrating effort. By 10a.m., three L.S.Ts had beached and thrown out pontoon causeways to connect with the solid ground. Later four others beached, but the receding tide prevented their pontoons from reaching the shore and unloading had to be delayed. The difficulty of developing the beach area was described in stark detail by Major Foreman:

"From the start the beach development was hampered by the very narrow area available between the dune-line and the road, and the terrific cratering in this small space and on the east side of the road. At high water mark there was no beach at all and at low water the beach, although 500 yards to 600 yards wide, was entirely useless as it consisted of thick black mud. The whole length of the beaches was faced from seaward with a sheer clay wall approximately 8 feet high; behind this was a 3 foot deep drain, then a space varying from 10 to 30 feet in width; a further drain approximately 3 feet deep, the road (of about 16 feet available width), another 3 foot drain, and then rising slopes of soft clay heavily pitted with water-filled craters. The road was also extensively cratered. The soil was of a thick greasy clay with the water table about one foot to 18 inches below the natural surface of the narrow coastal strip. Mechanical equipment was successfully landed from L.C.M's but for anything but the lightest cut quickly bogged itself down. Every dozer which attacked the clay wall bogged hopelessly and had to be dragged out by other mechanical equipment."

The tracked vehicles quickly made the mesh useless, but fortunately there was much round and sawn timber stacked on the beach and corduroy tracks were substituted. None of the L.S.T's

Tarakan Airfield. This picture gave Intelligence ample notice there were major problems with the uniform water-table.   AWM. 107035

Invasion Fleet   *2/3 Pioneer Ass.*

could be refloated on the afternoon tide. It had been hoped to have field guns in action on the island three hours after the landing, but unloading was so difficult that none was fired until 2.50 p.m. In the first twenty four hours, however, 1,562 tons of stores and equipment were unloaded.

Australian Liberators had been scheduled to make strikes on assault day, but failed to carry out the missions. Bostock was informed that they did not carry out their commitments because they had completed the allotted number of flying hours on which maintenance was based. This failure was severely criticised by him, and he said later:

> "In my opinion, it is inexcusable to allow consideration of routine maintenance procedure of this nature to preclude the employment of aeroplanes in operations in support of an assault on a beach-head."

On 2nd May a Liberator of the R.A.A.F. detailed for air observation duties over Tarakan failed to show up for the same reason. "Such inflexibility of effort," stated the R.A.A.F. Command report on the operation, "is intolerable, and could have caused acute operational embarrassment had the enemy ground opposition been more severe. Operations were resumed after inquiry into the cause of failure."

The principal objective was the airfield just over three miles to the north. The Dutch described it in glowing terms. The enemy strength was estimated at about 4000, it was later reviewed downwards to 1500 to 2000.

The task of taking the airfield was given to the 2/24 Bn. under Lt.Col. Warfe, an officer with a fine reputation who started his career with the 2/6 Bn. of the 6th Division. The two forward battalions, the 2/48 and 2/23, were soon ashore enlarging the bridgehead. After heavy fighting the airfield was taken on May 5. Accordingly the Brigade had kept to the first deadline of capturing the airfield. Full of confidence the R.A.A.F. Airfield Construction Squadron were now coming ashore cluttering up the restricted roads anxiously waiting to go into action. Officers inspected the field and found all the craters at a uniform water level and some of the lower levels of the strip covered by water.

Group Captain Rooney, the Commander of 61 Airfield Construction Squadron, knew he had problems – the rock which Spoor had claimed to have been there was mudstone which went to mud with traffic, frantically they began searching for gravel and sandstone; the coral NEFIS claimed to be available was no longer there. As material was located close to the front it was necessary to construct access roads and these also required road base – trucks collected rubble from destroyed buildings to repair and construct access to the new found sites, these could only be worked in daylight hours as the Japanese would have taken advantage of using the sound for movement cover. The problems compounded. The matting which was now ready to be unloaded was not sufficient to meet the requirements. Trucks were unable to use the strip for access as they damaged the strip surface. As the craters were filled the gravel went to mud and equipment bogged. Whitehead made his engineers available to assist with the problem – they pumped the craters out, lined them with material then filled them with reasonably dry road base – then the rain came –

No suitable road base was found until May 11, again, roads had to be constructed. Back at H.Q. estimates were called for completion dates – replies were despatched: 'If it doesn't rain and if suitable material is found....estimated dates ranged up to June 1' – too late to be sure about having aircraft to support OBOE 6 landing on Labuan on June 10.

In the meantime heavy fighting continued, the Japs were resisting fiercely as they realised there was no escape route. During this period Allied airforce attacks on the mainland of Borneo, Sandakan received a great deal of attention; the airfield there was no longer serviceable and most enemy airforce personnel had left. Allied reconnaissance reports indicated there were still some aircraft there, however, according to surviving POWs, Japanese aircraft were rare.

The Japanese at Sandakan were expecting an Allied assault at this time. General Baba, in January, ordered eight of his ten Battalions to move from the east coast to the west, there had been a constant movement of Jap troops along the road to Ranau. Colonel Otsuka, the C.O. of the Sandakan Garrison, moved his H.Q. back to Beluran, a distance of approximately 50 miles. The balance of his forces were dispersed in small groups around the Sandakan peninsula, and for some months natives had been busy cutting escape routes to the west. Sickness among the troops was causing many deaths, and most of the natives had already moved away to Libaran Island, which was organised by native leaders. Here fish and vegetables were available.

From the time the last of PYTHON party was picked up in June 1944 there was to be no interest in Borneo by the British-dominated S.R.D. until the AGAS parties were born in February 1945. In the meantime most of the intelligences coming out of Borneo came via Lt.Col. Suarez, Commander, Guerilla Forces Tawi Tawi.

Earlier in 1945 Suarez reported: "Loyal and patriotic natives of the western, northern and eastern coasts of Borneo have appealed and made representations to me for arms which they will use against the Japs there. They have unequivocally expressed their willingness to volunteer to fight and harass our common enemy there at even without pay.

"The Japs in Borneo are maltreating the civilians; confiscating their foodstuffs and property; and forcing them to work without compensation. They say that the Japs high-handed abuses are already unbearable and are ready to rise, revolt, and revenge!

"Recently, more than one thousand native refugees from Borneo coasts arrived at Sitangkai, Sulu, to take refuge from the Jap atrocities. Many more are arriving. To forestall food difficulties in Sulu which will surely ensue due to the great number of refugees seeking shelter here, it is strongly recommended that a shipment of arms and ammunition be sent us for use of the Borneo patriots. In this way they need not flock to Sulu for shelter and safety but could stay right in their home places in Borneo and fight for their homes and rights.

Waiting for Liberator raid on 'Helen' feature.   *2/3 Pioneer Ass.*

"Of course, I realize that Borneo is not within our territorial jurisdiction but, inasmuch as we are all fighting for a common cause, I believe that our war efforts should be co-ordinated as much as possible. Moreover, by organizing resistance forces there, we may be able, to a certain extent, cut off the flow of food supplies of the Japs from Borneo to Tawi Tawi, Sulu."

This letter was referred to General Berryman at Forward Echelon who noted: "The attached letter on "Request for Arms for use of Borneo Patriots" by Lt.Col. Alejandro Suarez of the Filipino Guerillas, dated 26 Jan '45, has been referred to me for an opinion by G-3 GHQ. As this involves a matter of policy and as British officials from British North Borneo are understood to be in Australia the matter is referred for a direction.

"As it is understood that AIB are interested in this area it might be better to await more definite information from AIB before making a decision. Furthermore the delivery of rifles to natives may draw the enemy's attention to areas which would not be in the interests of our future operations."

Once this reached the British no action was taken to arm the natives.

While heavy fighting continued on Tarakan plans were underway for the balance of the 9 Division to seize Labuan, Brunei Bay on June 10. This was to be followed by OBOE 2 Balikpapan on July 1. Both these operations were to be supported by the 1 TAC Airforce – planned to be operating out of Tarakan – however, at this time there seemed no hope the airfield would be serviceable. Fortunately the airfields seized during the VICTOR 4 Palawan and Tawi Tawi operations were now serviceable and able to support the current offensive.

The 26 Brigade was designated as the Reserve Force for both operations, planners believed Tarakan would be secured within two to three weeks, allowing the 2/3 Pioneer Battalion under Col. Anderson, together with Artillery and support troops to remain on garrison duty while the Brigade could be transferred for other duties for which shipping and support vessels would be in position for a pick-up. It seems if the 26 Brigade would not be needed to support either Balikpapan or North Borneo its most likely task would be to mount operations against Sandakan, Tawao and Lahat Datu, just to the north; however, stubborn resistance on the pear-shaped island was successfully holding down the Brigade. To be any help for those at Sandakan troops would have to be available by mid-May, and this was now out of the question – there were no Australian troops available in the 1st Australian Corps for such an operation. The

Australian Parachute Battalion back in Queensland would not be a sufficient force to conduct a rescue without considerable support which at this time was not available.

The PT Boat Command of the U.S. Seventh Fleet had now established a group of boats at Tawi Tawi, these were prowling along the North East Coast of Borneo like a pack of dogs, tearing away at any target in sight. This action, together with air strikes, had the Japanese off-balance and when the final attack came on May 27 precipitated the removal of the POWs.

There appears there was little coordination between A.I.B. and Air and Naval forces in connection with the presence of the POWs at Sandakan.

The United States Navy Support Ship POCOMOKE which sent the flying boat to rescue Owen Campbell.   *U.S. Navy*

Chapter 6

By May 16 the Brigade had lost 148 killed and 277 wounded and 243 were sick. It was the Infantry who suffered most of all. Only five prisoners were taken – the 2/3 Pioneer diarist reported:

"At this stage the first Japanese prisoner taken by the Pioneers was captured. He was spotted in 'C' Company's area as he crossed an open space. Everybody in the neighbourhood fired at him but he kept on running despite the tremendous weight of lead thrown at him and then he dropped.

"As soon as he did so a group of 'C' Company rushed him and found him unwounded but very frightened. He had fallen as much from hunger as from fear and exhaustion and one of his captors, instead of finishing him off, exclaimed: "The poor little bastard needs a feed!"

"The Jap propaganda had described the Australians as cannibals and there was no doubt that this fellow expected to be put in the pot, hence his dreadful fear. The Nip, immediately christened "Mickey Moto" was dragged to Company H.Q., given a feed and placed in the tender care of Sgt. Bill Gagie. From then he showed his appreciation for not being eaten, as once he fully expected to have been, by following the worthy sergeant around like a dog and when finally he had to leave his custodian he was almost in tears."

It was obvious planners anticipated a campaign lasting two to three weeks. The Brigade had landed with 19,500 rounds and now guns were restricted to 500 rounds per day and were relying on support from the B24s with 500 and 1000 pounders together with Lightnings with napalm. The island features were sharp clay ridges with ample timber available; the Japanese made good use of the terrain for tunnel network which was difficult for the Infantry to dislodge.

The plan now was for the Infantry to pull back from highly defended positions, mark the target with smoke bombs and call in the B24s. A formation of 18 bombers from the 13 A.A.F. carrying a heavy load would appear over the island and, in consultation with the Artillery Air Liaison officer, would identify the target. While this approach was most effective, delays occurred owing to weather conditions and it was not always the bombers could meet the schedule required by Brigade.

By June G.H.Q. must have been growing concerned at the delay in occupying the island – 46 Liberators were used in one assault. It is difficult to understand the claim that Tarakan was strategically important when the facts are examined. The airfield was unserviceable, the Japanese possessed only a few aircraft in Borneo and no ships. The claim seemed to be made to cover up the embarrassment of the failure in using Tarakan as it was intended, a base for the Tactical Airforce to support operations against Brunei Bay, British North Borneo and Balikpapan, principal oil port in Dutch Borneo.

Air Commodore Scherger, commenting on the Tarakan operation after the war, said: "It is perhaps true that OBOE 1 was a failure on the part of the R.A.A.F but one must qualify this by saying that the

Well fed and dressed Japanese Prisoners of War at Tarakan.

task set was impossible of achievement by any Airforce; against this it is equally true to say that we continued to base our plans for air support of OBOE 6 (Labuan-Brunei Bay) and OBOE 2 (Balikpapan) on the operation of attack and fighter types from Tarakan, and it was quite obvious (at least to myself and those of my staff who visited there) that a satisfactory strip could never be constructed, nor indeed could a strip be made, capable of intensive use for even a short period."

Tarakan was a victory for the Dutch – in a matter of weeks they had some of the oil wells in production. The chances of having forces available to seize Sandakan while the prisoners were there had now disappeared.

While there were conflicting reports emanating from A.I.B. as to the real status of the POWs there, L.H.Q. sent S.E.A.C. Command a telegram, dated 22 June, in part:

Men of the 9th Division were shocked to learn Lt. Tom Derrick, V.C., D.C.M., 2/48Bn. had died of wounds on May 24, 1945. Members of his platoon helped carry him to Casualty Clearing, one of whom was Mark Wells. That night, Mark's brother Frank was killed and next day buried next to Derrick. Padre Bryson conducted the service   *AWM.44970*

118

"........ at Sandakan 1 June 500 Australian/British POWs moved westward from POW Camp which was destroyed by Japs. 150 POW too sick to walk remained. Fate not known. Prisoners dropping out on march shot........these POW believed now in vicinity Beluran or Labuk Bay. Effort made to contact."

The message explains why there were sudden changes in the direction of AGAS parties now in the Labuk Bay area — they commenced movements which were designed to intercept or be close enough to give assistance if the opportunities arose.

It was known the first party of POWs left Sandakan for Ranau late January and confirmed reports there were about 300 who had arrived at Ranau, now it was known the balance of those able to march were destined for Ranau.

Major Rex Blow, who had distinguished himself as leader of the Filipino Guerillas when they captured the Japanese stronghold of Malabang in April 1945, had now joined `Z' Special Unit and was anxious to see if he could help his mates at Sandakan. He was taken by U.S. PT boat to Libaran Island at the entrance to Lubuk Bay where he conferred with local natives, together with a frightened guide he was dropped off west of Sandakan where he intercepted the rentis; he found there had been recent traffic but no sign of POWs.

After a few days he was picked up and returned to Libaran Island where he met up with Lt. Hollingsworth on July 2, 1945, he informed him he had met up with a native who stated he was working for the Japanese and that he was on duty guarding coolies walking from mile 17 to 42 and when he met the party there were also a hundred plus white prisoners. But they were very weak and sick and he stated there were only four left when they reached mile 42. These were most probably shot as several reports stated 4 white prisoners were seen about that time in the vicinity but no further news was heard of them.

Blow would be referring to what was known as the 'third march', the Japanese stated there were 75 in this group. Finally Blow stated:

"Reports gathered from many sources indicate there are NO POWs left in the area, and a great percentage of those previously here have died of sickness or have been callously shot."

A.I.B. were now piecing together the whereabouts of the POWs; an officer was spending as much time as Dick Braithwaite could bear gaining information on the movements and condition of the POWs up to the time of his escape from the second march. Blow's report indicated there were no prisoners of war at Sandakan.

183 of the 536 who left on the second march had now reached Ranau on June 26, one Australian was carried in dead. Here they were shocked to learn there were only six survivors from the 470 who left Sandakan in late January 1945, one wonders if the starvation program had not been introduced in April 1944 but deferred until late 1944 or early 1945 how many prisoners would have made Ranau. It seems the "kill the prisoners" program was well known to Major Watanabe at Ranau; Takakuwa stated: "In the course of a conversation with Col. Otsuka on 27 May 1945 before I left Sandakan, he mentioned that under the present conditions it would be inadvisable to leave any POWs behind while marching to Ranau. Far better that they should be disposed of as they would be in the way of any fighting that took place along the track. On many occasions prior to this Col. Otsuka had expressed the opinion that it would be better if all POWs are dead.

"When I reported to Major Watanabe Yoshio on my arrival at Ranau and he learned that the POWs would be of no value for working parties he expressed the opinion that it would be better if the POWs at Ranau were to die off quickly implying that they might be assisted to die. I told him that they were receiving 100 gms of rice per day at the moment and that this was not enough for them to work on. I suggested increasing the ration to 300 gms per day but he said that they had already tried that before on the Ranau POWs and they were still unable to work on it. He therefore refused my request to increase the ration."

Earlier, G.H.Q. approved an Intelligence party being inserted to establish a base on the east coast of British North Borneo. Its objectives were to establish wireless communication with Australia, (ii) to set up a native intelligence network with particular attention focussed on the POW Camp at Sandakan and the high priority target Kudat, (iii) and through Agents establish friendly relations with the natives and ultimately organise such armed resistance as might be authorised by G.H.Q.

This party was designated AGAS 1 under the command of Major Chester who, since late 1943, was anxious to get to the west coast of Borneo. The party comprised Capt. D.S. Sutcliffe, Lt. Don Harlem, Lt. F.G. Olsen, Sgt. Greenwood, Sgt. Wong Sue and Cpl. Hywood.

Major Chester felt it was necessary to have a closer look at the area. A request was lodged for an aircraft to carry out a reconnaissance of the whole of the Sandakan Peninsula and Labuk Bay. On 13 February a B24 was provided from Leyte and Major Chester and Major Combe flew over the locality and took photographs of the entire waterfront, airfield and possible drop

Cpl. John Bernard McKay, NX.20317, V.C. 2/3 Pioneer Bn. Killed in Action Tarakan May 12, 1945. With his Section on the 'Helen' feature he charged three machine gun positions holding up his platoon advance, bayonetting one gunner then killed the crew of the second gun with grenades. During this action McKay killed 7 Japs and silenced 3 machine guns. McKay was killed in this action. Following a heavy bombardment of the 'Helen' feature a fighting patrol under Lt. Hewlett was sent to report on the aftermath of the bombing. He sent a wireless message: "I'm up Helen Hill" which was heard as far away as Morotai. 2/3 Pioneer Ass.

zones, and special attention was paid to water craft which could interfere with the operation.

When Chester returned to Base he sent a signal (26 February 1945) requesting air strikes on all the water craft and launches seen in the area. Prior to 3-4 March these were the only craft which could interfere with the forthcoming insertion of AGAS party, now set for the above date.

On 24 February, the USS TUNA (Capt. Stefanides, USN) got underway from Darwin to conduct the special mission to insert the party under Chester into Labuk Bay just north of Sandakan. The TUNA sighted an island where they remained in the vicinity in order to fix their position for the submerged run into Labuk Bay. They reached a predetermined point in 9 fathoms, just 5-1/2 miles off shoreline, manned battle stations and commenced unloading. At 2058 hours the AGAS party left the ship in darkness on a calm sea and landed near an unnamed river 1$1/2$ miles off Kg. Tagahan. The TUNA silently left the area.

The party landed at daylight on March 4, between Pagaham and Puru Puru Island, and moved inland some two miles, where a small

Lt. Don Harlem's party.   *Vic Kelm*

camp was made becoming Base 1. Communication was established to H.Q. S.R.D. immediately.

They made folboat sorties along the coast, seeking native contacts and making an initial recce of the area. On 1 April 1945 contact was established at Jamboagan Island village, the natives were strongly anti-Japanese. Major Chester, Capt. Sutcliffe, Lt. Harlem held a conference with the natives and Abdul Rajak, village Hadji, and they all showed their willingness to co-operate and requested they be given arms to use against the Japanese. This island was the collecting point for refugee natives from the coast area.

Captain Sutcliffe decided to establish a semi-permanent H.Q. at Jamboagan, and moved the complete party in on April 3. They began to recruit and train a guerilla force and establish an intelligence network for information and assistance in the defence of the Base. Information was received that the party's presence was known to the enemy, so the village was set in a state of defence.

The first stores drop took place on April 20, with further supply drops on April 28 and May 3, when Phase Two of the party arrived under Major Combe. In a matter of three weeks Chester claimed to have established a wide network of agents and described having supplied reliable information on the Japanese withdrawal from the east coast and the move of the POWs at Sandakan to Ranau.

On 20 May 1945, Major Chester was extracted by Catalina and taken to Morotai for de-briefing. The unsigned report details the evidence of further Japanese withdrawals from the east coast and further weakening of Japanese strength in the Sandakan area and identifies the track to Ranau, the principal escape route; it concludes with a paragraph, "Miscellaneous" : "All POWs have now been moved from Sandakan to Ranau, where they are now. Many were killed or died on the way, and no estimate can be given at the moment of their numbers or their location at Ranau. When they were in transit they were not allowed to converse with natives, but when halted at stopping places they could talk freely with the local people." At the time this report was made there were about 900 prisoners of war still in the camp at Sandakan –

Major Chester returned to Jambongan on 25 May with information which caused a change in policy. Major Chester would have been told while at Morotai there was no foreseeable date they could forecast when elements of the 26 Brigade at Tarakan would be available to seize Sandakan. The plan was now to strike out strongly at the Japs causing as much damage and casualties as possible and to intensify the search for information further west.

With this new policy, Captain Sutcliffe changed his plans and with his small force of partially trained guerillas he decided to strike at the Japanese on the west.

Lt. Hollingsworth was inserted by Catalina on May 27. Sutcliffe decided to leave him at Jambongan and move inland to the Sungei Sungei area with the balance of the party and establish a base on the Sugut River. This move took place on 29 May, the force was divided into two parties – Sutcliffe moving via Paitan and Harlem via Trusan. Major Chester, now AGAS 111, took a small party to Koumanis Bay area from May 29 to June 7, 1945. This party was inserted by a Catalina of 113 Air Sea Rescue Squadron (Flt. Lt. Gregson) south of the Boogawan River on 29 May and included Sgt. Wong Sue (Jack Sue), Cpl. Hywood and Mandon Ali.

Sutcliffe reached Sungei Sungei without incident, but Harlem came into contact with the Japs at Trusan on 30 May. There were 12 Japs guarding a considerable amount of stores, food and medical supplies; the Japs evacuated Trusan hurriedly and Harlem's party destroyed all enemy stores in the village then came on to Sungei Sungei. The Japs at Sandakan would have run at the same speed if attacked.

Sutcliffe now planned to continue to operate with two forces. The first party moving to Lingkabau then to Telupid on the Labuk River to harass the Japs in this area and to obtain information re POWs in Sandakan. The second party, under Lt. Harlem, was to move via Lingkabau to Meridi area with a similar task. Both groups would then be astride the two main Jap east-west lines of communication to Ranau. As Hollingsworth and one Signaller remained at Jambongan, it meant the force was short of a Signaller for this plan but, in response to signals to H.Q., Signaller Kelm was inserted into Sungei Sungei on 7 June and Sutcliffe's plan could now proceed. Just as well the drop zone was in friendly hands as Signaller Kelm landed in a tree and the natives below were members of the guerilla force.

Thirty enemy were reported to be garrisoned in the village of Aling and, after an initial reconnaissance to confirm this, Harlem and Sutcliffe, with 23 guerillas, attacked. The operation was completely successful and the village was captured intact after a fierce fire fight. Eleven Japs were killed and one later found to have escaped. Sutcliffe's guerilla losses due to enemy action were one killed and one seriously wounded, but they suffered more from desertions which further prevented him from using his original idea of two forces.

Sutcliffe was now ready to proceed with his plan to harass the

Japanese on their two main escape routes to the west when he got word the Japs were aware of their presence and had despatched a larger force in their direction; he now made plans to move to Bangaya where H.Q. was established on June 14.

Sutcliffe received reports from Kulang of the Muanad district and a further request from H.Q. as to whether he could confirm the information forwarded by Chester on May 20 that there were no POWs left at Sandakan. He had now received information as to the movement of POWs along the routes in the Muanad area and he replied he was unable to confirm the report of Major Chester.

The day the OBOE 6 convoy left Morotai for Brunei Bay Brigadier Wells, B.G.S. of the 1 Aust. Corp. sent a Top Secret request to Brigadier Wills, Controller of Allied Intelligence Bureau, seeking detailed report on the Ranau area to be furnished within two or three weeks. Corp. H.Q. were now investigating what action could be taken to rescue the prisoners believed to have been concentrated at Ranau. They were aware of the number who had left Sandakan and according to their reports there could have been about 300 alive. They were now desperate for more detailed information.

They required the number and locality of Japanese strength together with weapon strength such as AA Guns, Artillery machine guns and mortars and their routine in addition to the number of POWs and their guards, their arms, where they were held and the type of fence around the compound. They were anxious to know if guerillas were active in the area and whether they could be concentrated to assist. The details of the local airstrip, its soil composition, type of surface and availability of material for repair of the strip.

H.Q. were obviously planning an airborne rescue of the prisoners. The 1st Aust. Para. Bn. was still uncommitted back in Queensland and could be brought forward if the plan became feasible.

Plans were soon finalised for AGAS 111 to be inserted into North Borneo to provide the information required. The party was under Flt. Lt. Ripley (R.A.A.F.), Sgt. A.W.C. Hywood, A.I.F. Sigs., P.C. Sampura, P.C. Ampun, P.C. Jahil and O.T. Andong Ajak.

They were taken to Jambongan where they went to Melobong by boat and proceeded by foot to Pitas. They left there on July 8, 1945 and arrived at Melinsau on July 16 and later moved to Kiayip to receive an urgent food drop which they collected on July 25.

Believing Merugin to be occupied by the enemy, they by-passed it and carried on to Lansat after a five day journey arriving on 2 August. Gimbahn brought information that W.O. Sticpewich and

Herman Reither were living in the jungle west of Ranau.

This was the break the A.I.B. needed urgently – someone to provide information on the conditions and number of POWs still alive at Ranau. They now feared the worst, by the end of June they were able to talk to Dick Braithwaite who escaped from the second march – he would have given them the number of dead back at Sandakan and he would have known better than anyone as he had engraved their names on metal tags to be placed on the graves. Within a few weeks Owen Campbell was rescued and picked up by Mariner flying boat.

Sticpewich had named almost all those alive on July 28 when he had escaped with Reither. Takahara, the friendly Formosan, had seen the written orders detailing the order of killing. Capt. Takakuwa, who was suffering from malaria, would not have been very tolerant when he was advised the acting camp leader had escaped.

The massacre was delayed while searches went on for Sticpewich and Reither, finally, on August 1, 1945, the last of the survivors were murdered.

Capt. Cook guarded the Nominal Rolls, through the years he meticulously recorded the date of death of each man. Finally, when he was too ill to continue, he handed them to Lt. Watanabe with the request they be forwarded to the Allies. Watanabe Genzo, the officer who supervised the killing of those abandoned, destroyed the evidence, however that did not save him from the firing squad.

In the meantime, Sgts. Neil and Russell reached the Nelapak area where they had come across the bodies of Australians – some partly buried, some just covered by their ground sheet – the Aussie slouch hat, a symbol of courage and determination – the brown-covered paybooks showing stains of sweat, moisture from the harsh years of their owner's survival, together with snapshots of family – they would have been the most treasured and guarded possessions of the prisoners and they would have been clutched to the end.

On August 18, 1945, the R.A.A.F. dropped leaflets, signed by General Blamey, along the road to Ranau, telling the dead the Japanese Emperor Hirohito, who enunciated the policies to be adopted towards POWs, had accepted the terms of the Potsdam Declaration. They fluttered down upon the bodies and graves of the Australians who were abandoned –

U.S.S. TUNA   *U.S. Navy*

Lt. Hollingsworth and Sig. Vic Kelm with guerilla forces on Jambongan Island.   *Vic Kelm*

Chapter 7

General Blamey's claim that the prisoners at Sandakan could have been rescued if G.H.Q. South West Pacific had made transport aircraft available was made when speaking to the Armoured Division Reunion in Melbourne in 1947.

It is not known what prompted this statement when earlier he had written to a friend and stated: "The allocation of Australian troops to operations is entirely the responsibility of General MacArthur, and I have no real say in the matter beyond carrying out the orders received. While I have pretty strong feelings on certain of these allocations I have no right to criticise them."

Blamey fully understood the situation regarding the prisoners at Sandakan and would have urged General Berryman, Chief of Staff at Allied Land H.Q., to place his concern before those at G.H.Q. He surely would have known precisely what G.H.Q.s intentions were when he told Rex Blow in April 1945 when Blow and McLaren asked what about our mates in Sandakan, and his reply to them was: "If a rescue can be fitted into forthcoming operations it will be done – and both of you will be involved."

Blamey would have understood better than anyone much depended on the successful conclusion of the OBOE operation before a large scale rescue of those at Sandakan could be considered. Sandakan, according to G.H.Q. assessments, was well down the list of priorities and probably lower because of the presence of prisoners of war. The occupation of Kuching where there were some 2000 POWs and Internees was at the bottom of the list of priorities for General Morshead.

When 'Kingfisher' proposal was submitted to G.H.Q. for examination MacArthur was deeply involved with the capture of the

Philippines in accordance with plans prepared by the Joint Chiefs of Staff; it is unlikely the proposal would have reached a higher level – the occupation would have taken place some time after Tarakan, Balikpapan and Brunei Bay, when any rescue would have been too late.

The principal cause of the fate of the prisoners was the deliberate policy of starvation and withholding of medical supplies. This order first became effective in 1942 when Prime Minister Tojo decreed the 'No work No food' policy towards prisoners of war and issued orders for their dispersement to work on military projects, contrary to Hague and Geneva Conventions. The order further decreed that sick prisoners received a reduced ration – this policy affected all Nationalities in all areas of Asia. The isolated instance when the Australian Red Cross representative in Singapore was arrested and charged by the Japanese with financing involvement in an ill-conceived and irresponsible action for two officers to arrange an aircraft through the Chinese and fly to India! They all ended up in the notorious Outram Road Gaol – the local Japanese cited this incident as the reason for the discontinuing of Red Cross supplies after 1942.

A proposal was submitted to the Japanese for a scheme to purchase food from the natives whereby payment would be made at the cessation of hostilities – this was rejected.

The Japanese treated Allied prisoners with absolute contempt. When Southern Command were informed there was a POW sign displayed on the ground at the camp they ordered it be removed as it may offer some advantage to the Allies. This action seemed to confirm their fear of an airborne assault there.

After the capture of the three Australians of PYTHON the Japanese fear of an airborne invasion became real, reinforcements were called for to protect the airfield and adjacent area suitable for drop zones.

There were a number of reductions in rations from March, however, the most severe cut was made in June. The contention is, if the presence of PYTHON had not been discovered, reduction of food may not have been made until late October when the bombing commenced. There could have been several hundred prisoners still alive at Ranau at the cessation of hostilities.

Any proposal to secure Sandakan prior to March 1945 was not practical. An invasion could have been successful in conjunction with the VICTOR 4 operations at the time when General Eichelberger's Task Force was occupying Palawan and Tawi Tawi, just 100 miles away; however, despite the success of the Los Banos operation being the relief of the last concentration of internees in the Philippines, G.H.Q. would have considered the possible repercussions on those 2000 POWs and Internees at Kuching and decided against such a move.

The possibility of Sandakan being relieved if the OBOE 1 had not been changed from Jesselton to Tarakan when shipping and aircraft were in place, there was a real chance that many prisoners could have been saved. However the change to Tarakan meant it would be months before the relief of Sandakan could be considered. In the meantime the death rate increased and condition of the prisoners deteriorated rapidly.

After the capture of Tawi Tawi and the establishment of a Motor Torpedo Boat Command Sandakan was constantly attacked by sea as Allied aircraft continued to attack native houses as the only remaining targets. The Japanese, expecting an invasion, panicked and General Baba ordered the prisoners moved to Ranau.

Left: Gnr. Kenneth Allan McIlroy, NX.7338. Greenwich, NSW. Died 25 July 1945 Ranau. Margaret McIlroy.

Right: Pte. Neil Tipping, NX.44279. Crows Nest, NSW. Died Ranau 4 July 1945 – mate of Ken McIlroy. Margaret McIlroy.

Left: Dvr. Earnest James Percival, QX.16818. Goondiwindi, Qld. Died Sandakan 25 February 1945. Phil Percival

Right: Pte. Clarence Alexander Grinter. VX.55109. Nathalia, Vic. Went to Borneo July 1942. Died 28 March 1945. Father of 5 daughters and 1 son. Val Kenelly

Chapter 8

"For the past 40 odd years I have wondered just what happened and where my Dad was. I only remember this tall man in this resplendent soldier's uniform standing with his back to the old wood stove and how proud a 4 year old boy was of his Dad" ...wrote Phil Percival of Goondiwindi when he first learned, in 1989, that his father had died at Sandakan in 1945. "Mum had a couple of early letters saying how well he was getting looked after but then to all accounts he disappeared off the face of the earth. I can remember as if it only happened yesterday the look of hope on my Mother's face as the mailman stopped at the gate but he never had a letter. As the years went by of course we all prayed for a miracle and that one day soon he would come striding through the door as only a 10ft. tall Dad in a child's eyes can do but as always miracles like that never happen. Around 1945 Mum received the usual letter saying he was missing presumed dead. She never told us (I have 2 brothers) but we did sense from the sadness you could feel in the old house it was all over but of course no one ever asked.

"For all these years especially around Anzac Day and Christmas I used to wonder what life would have been like with a father, I used to notice the special bond between a father and son. Probably knowing not when he died or where, was the annoying thing. I did talk to a returned soldier once who was on the Burma railway and he seemed to remember a Percival so over all these years I assumed he died on the Burma railway but when Mrs. Doolin rang me it was as if a huge weight had been taken away. Dad's name and serial number and his death 25th February 1945. Now of course there is anger that he survived all the hell for all those years and only a few more months would have seen him home.....I must confess to a few tears as I write this letter but we who did not experience the torture and hell you went through can never know what it was like not even in our most frightening nightmares, yet you were willing to endure these torments to tell us the story. Thank you. I don't know whether you believe in the supernatural, perhaps it was only the fervent desire to have him back home but as little children I often heard Mum and my Grandmother call out, 'Is that you Ernie?' We all heard heavy footsteps (he used to wear those great big old boots) on the verandah. This happened quite a few times in the middle of the night. Maybe it was him yearning for home, who knows. One morning, and it was towards the war's end, my Grandmother told us she hardly slept, she kept dreaming of Dad fighting a huge snake. She said he was calling for help but she couldn't get to him. Maybe that was when the bastards killed him....."

"It's the not knowing that kills you", said Fay Freeman, one of Clarrie Grinter's six children, when she wrote. "I was only 7 years old when my beloved father left for 'over there'. As the war progressed, we wrote letters, sent photos, learned to knit socks. Mum made endless fruit cakes which she put into a cake tin called a "soldiers tin" then the tin was sewed up inside canvas and sent to Dad via the 'Red Cross' who it was said would make sure it was delivered along with the socks. The only correspondence we received in 3½ years was two cards bearing "Japanese" characters and a short message which read "No letters or photograph yet"........ I have nothing but my early childhood memories and a photograph to show who my father was. The Army telegram said "Died P.O.W. March 28th 1945." My family were led to believe malaria or beri-beri, at the time no information was available from the Army, somehow I always thought that it was the death march. It was a week before my twelfth birthday when the news came the war was over and we were expecting him home."

Jacqueline Tolnay, daughter of Sgt. Jack Gaven who died at Ranau, wrote:"........I knew my father was a POW but news did not come very often. The worst fact is not knowing what really happened. All conjectures give no comfort, when a loved one disappears without trace. All sorts of fantasies have crossed my mind........and the thought that our lives would have been different if our father had returned – not necessarily better but different. It's a rare day that passes without thinking of my father with sadness, but fondly too."

Tom Connolly was only five when his father, Corporal T.W.J. Connolly, went away: "My father stood me on the lounge chair in our home at Randwick and told me he was going away and I was to look after Mum. Later, Mum said he was a prisoner of war, which I never really understood what it really meant, but the feeling in the house was he would be out of danger. The family seemed more

Left: Cpl. Thomas William Joseph Connolly, NX.51283. Last reported in camp at Ranau July 28, 1945. Killed August 1, 1945.

Tom Connolly.

Right: Gnr. Finlay Cameron, QX.8427. Mackay Qld. Died Sandakan 7 June 1945. Identity discs and shoulder Australias found. F. Cameron

Left: Pte. John Barrie, NX.68426. During World War 1 his three brothers served overseas, he was married with a young family and looked after the farm. At the outbreak of World War 11, determined to serve, he put his age back 10 years, enlisted and was sent to Malaya 1941. His eldest daughter looked after the farm. He died 15 June 1945 at Sandakan, aged 56. E. Voorwinden.

Right: Spr. John McFarlane, WX.7227. Leederville, W.A. When John's youngest brother, Clem, enlisted the Recruiting Officer said: "You're the second McFarlane to come in today – you better get back in line and come back 21." From a broken home, Clem met John for the first time in 14 years. Now destined for Borneo he hoped to meet John there – the 9 Div. sailed past Sandakan on June 8-9 – John died Sandakan June 20, 1945 Carol Vince

concerned about Uncle Jack who was reported 'Missing Believed Prisoner of War'. My Grandparents were traditional Roman Catholics and between us we said many Hail Marys for the safe return of my father and uncle. One morning my Mother told my sister and me of our father's death, the previous night I had overheard Grandmother telling a neighbour of his death. News of Uncle Jack's death arrived about the same time (Jack Cleary, H.Q. Coy. 2/20 Bn. Killed at Kranji 9.2.42).

"The war was over, there was little joy in our house – I remember going into the back lane and lying down and having a good cry."

Acknowledgments

My Thanks to:

Tim Bowden, the A.B.C. Social History Department, for access to transcripts of 'Prisoners of War Under Nippon'.

George Blaikie A.M. for his professional guidance.

Alex Dandie for access to his Records Collection.

Major Rex Blow, D.S.O., Mentioned in Despatches, for his contributions.

Major Ray Steele, D.S.O., who also escaped from Berhala Island and was later evacuated by the USS NARWHAL to Australia in March 1944.

The Staff of the Records Collection, Australian War Memorial, Canberra, particularly Bill Fogarty, Ron Gilchrist and Bronwyn Self.

The Staff of the Australian Archives in Canberra and Brighton, Victoria, for their prompt and helpful assistance.

Major Bill Jinkins, M.B.E., Bronze Star (U.S.), of PYTHON, for his contribution of photographs and detail of his involvement.

Lindsay Cottee, Mentioned in Despatches, Phase 1, PYTHON and Stan Neil, Mentioned in Despatches, Phase 11, PYTHON for kind use of their Memoirs.

Patrick C. Parsons of Manila, son of the famous Commander Charles Parsons who was MacArthur's man in the Philippines 1943-1945.

Bob Marchant of The Mindanao Guerillas Association, California, for the records of this Association.

Jack Samples of California – a mate of Blow and McLaren.

Major General C.H. Finlay, (Retd.) C.B., C.B.E., O.B.E., M.I.D., who was G.S.O.1 to General Berryman, Chief of Staff Forward Land H.Q.

for his information on the "Kingfisher" proposal.

Dennis Pidhayney, 20th Air Force Association, California, who produced Bessie Sneed's book for me.

Wes Bentley and 2/3 Pioneer Battalion Association for pictures and access to their Tarakan history. The late Vic Kelm of Warracknabeal and of AGAS who was there when Owen Campbell was rescued, who provided pictures of Jambongan.

Bob Piper of the R.A.A.F. Historical Department for the photo of Sqdr. Ldr. Peter Jeffrey.

W.A.C. Russell of 'Z' Special Unit who was with the first POW Investigation and Enquiry Group into Sandakan October 1945.

Sincere thanks to the family members of those lost in Sandakan who are mentioned in the text for their courage in telling of that time and of how they faced the tragedy which shattered so many of their hopes and dreams, for their letters and family photographs.

And to the many others who have assisted, including Peter Gorrick, Mark Wells, Jack Cannon, Clem Seale for his Artist's contribution depicting the events of May 27, 1945, used on the Cover Jacket of the book.

To the Operational Archives Branch, Department of the Navy, Naval Historical Centres, Washington, U.S.A. for the supply of United States submarine details and photographs.

The Office of Information, Department of the Navy, Washington, U.S.A. for information on Commander Charles Parsons and the U.S. Guerilla Forces in Mindanao.

James M. Kendall, 13th U.S. Airforce Historian, for photographs.

Lt. Col. H.W.S. Jackson, Keith Botterill, Owen Campbell, Nelson Short and Frank Hole.

And my thanks to the many friends who picked up the phone to answer my queries.

Don Wall

References Used

Australian Archives
   Report by Justice Barry. (CP389/1/1 Item BUN.1)
   Various Reports – A32691

Australian War Memorial
   Brief History of G.2 Section G.H.Q., S.W.P.A. (AWM.59)

Bergamini, David
   Imperial Conspiracy

Blair, Clay, Jnr.
   Silent Victory

Dysett, Edward Adamson, H.C.
   Guerilla Submarines

Gill, G. Hermon
   Royal Australian Navy 1942-45

Hetherington, John
   Blamey

Keats, John
   They Fought Alone

Long, Gavin
   The Final Campaign

Mindanao Guerillas Association – Marchant, L.
   Records – Mindanao

Odgers, George
   The Air War Against Japan 1943-45

Sneed, Bessie
   Captured by the Japanese

Smith, Robert Ross
    U.S. Army in World War 11 – Triumph in the Philippines

United States Army Air Force
    Historical Volume No. 111

Wall, Donald
    Sandakan – The Last March
    Singapore and Beyond

* * * *

INDEX

Abin, Policeman	70,71,73,74
AGAS	112,119,120,122,124,125
Ahong	78
Ampun, P.C.	125
Anderson, Pte.	11
Andong, Ajak	125
Arthur, Group Captain	104
Baba, Lieut General	7,96,98,112,130
Bariga	11
Barrie, Pte. J.	134
Barry, J.V. K.C.	105
Bayau (Native)	62
Berryman, Lieut General	91,114,128
Blow, Major R.	24,25,26,27,40,119,120,128
Blamey, General Sir T.	28,31,91,94,106,126,128
BLUEFIN, USS	47
Bostock, Air Vice Marshal	104,105,110
Botterill, Pte. K.	10
Bowler, Captain	24
Braithwaite, Bdr. R.	11,99,120,126
Brandis, Sgt. W.	40,41,42,50,69
Broadhurst, Captain	30,35,43
Brinkman, L/Cpl. J.	3
Brown, S/Sgt. R.G.	8
Butler, DVR.	24,26,27
Cain, Lt.	30,40,44,50
Cameron, Gnr. F.	134
Campbell, Gnr. Owen	2,3,11,68,98,126

Chave, General	91,92
Chester, Major (Gort)	30,31,34,36,37,38,39,40,42,43,44, 48, 50,51,54,55,56,61,62,66,98,120, 122,123,124,125
Chew, W.O.A.	40,45,54,55,56
Chien Pei	73,74
Chiang Kai Chek	61
Christie, Admiral	50,66
Cleary, Pte. J.	135
Cobby, Air Commodore	104
Combe, Major	122,123
Connolly, Cpl. J.W.J.	133,134
Cook, Captain G	6,68,83,126
Cottee, Sgt. L.L.	35,36,39,42,43,48,56,57,58
Curtin, Mr. J. Hon.	14
Datu Mohammed, Moro Leader	27
Dallessandro, V.L. TMIC USN	53
Dealey, Cdr. S.D. (Sam)	47,51,60
Derrick, Lt. T. V.C.	118
Dodds, Sgt. S.	50,51,53,54,55,56,66
Drakeford, A. Hon.	105
Dyess, Lt.Col.	22,24
Egami Sobei (Judge)	75
Eichelberger, General	92,129
Esler, Lt.	75
Ewin, Lt.	75
Fertig, Lt.Col. Wendell	16,18,19,20,22,23,24,26,27,28,29, 30,87,88
Foreman, Major	108
Funk, Alex	70,71
Gagie, Sgt. W.	116
Galton, Lt. D.	7
Gaven, Sgt. J.	133
Gillon, Lt. M.	24,25,26,27
Gibson, Group Captain	104
Grashio, Sam	22
Greenwood, Sgt.	120
Gregson, Flt.Lt.	124
Grinter, Pte. C.	97,131,133
GUDGEON, USS	19

HADDO, USS	47,60
Hamner, Capt. J.	19,20,27,30,37,38,40,44,50,51,61
HARDER, USS	47,51,52,53,57,60,66
Harlem, Lt. D.	120,122,124
Harvey, Pte.	26
Hayashi, Lt.Col.	91
Haye, Pt.	9
Hedges, Lt.Col. Charles	16,18,24,28
Heath, General	35
Hewlett, Lt.	121
Hirohito, Emperor	15,126
Hollingsworth, Lt. 'Jock'	119,124, 127
Honey, Wing Commander	104
Honma, General	15,16
Hoshijima, Capt. Susumu	5,7,10,25,26,68,69,70,83,87,93, 96,97
Hywood, Cpl.	120,124,125
Ichikawa, Japanese Q.M.	5
Isamu Miura (Interpreter)	41,46
Jahil, P.C.	125
Jaria (Native)	41
Jeffrey, Captain R.	9,86
Jeffrey, Sqdn.Ldr. P.	86
Jinkins, Major W.	30,31,40,43,44,47,48,50,51,53, 55,56,61,66
Johnstone, Major	75
Jones, Air Vice Marshal	104,105
Joo Ming	5
Kanazawa, Lt.	75
Keith, Mrs. Agnes	7
Kelm, Sig. V.	124,127
Kenny, General G.	105
Kendall, James	81
Kent, Pte. R.	75
Kennedy, Pte. J.	24,26,30,31
King, General	15
Kingfisher Operation	32,85,90,93,128
KINGFISH, USS	35,36
Knudsen, Tor	28
Kulang, Orang Tuan	7 ,9, 10, 125
Kuroda, Warrant Officer (IJA)	41,46

Koram, Corporal	26,26
Kwok, Dr. A.	38,40,43,61,62
Latta, Lt.Cdr. F. (USN)	29,30,31
Laureto, Captain	22
Lai Kueifu, Nurse	71
Los Banos Agricultural College	94,95
Lim Keng Fatt	38,43,62,64,66
Lowrance, Capt. (USN)	36
Maginal	71
Maeda, Lt.Col.	75,77
Mandor Alam	41
Mandor Ali	124
Matusap	70
Matsuii Kioshi	46
Matsumoto, Capt.	75,77,78
Matthews, Capt. M.C.	5,6,69,70,72,73,74,75,79
Mavar, Mr.	73,74
Mellnik, Major	22,23,24,88
Mills, Capt. (UK)	68
Morshead, General Sir L.	102,105,128
Mosher, Capt.	83
Moxham, Bdr.	11
Morgan, Luis	18
MacArthur, General D.	13,14,15,16,18,19,20,21,29,60, 61,67,88,91,92,93,94,96,100, 102,128
McCollum, Capt (US GHQ)	47,50
McCoy, Cdr. Melvin	21,23,24
McFarlane, Spr. J.	134
McGill, Pte. L.	8
McGlinn, Gnr. A.J.	8
McIlroy, Bdr. K.A.	131
McKenzie, Sgt. D.G.	40,45,46,47,50,69,79
McKay, Sig. T.R.B.	8,26
(s/a McKenzie, D.S.)	
McKay, Cpl. B. V.C.	121
McLaren, Pte. R.K. later Capt.	24,25,26,27,106,128
McLish, Lt. Col.	22,24
McMillan, Cpl.	74
MIS.X	88
"Mickey Moto" (Jap.prisoner)	116
Nagai, Capt. Hirowa	10,93,94

Nagita, 1st Lt.	77
NARWHAL, USS	29,30,31,44,50,61,88
NAUTILUS, USS	29
Neil, Sgt. S.	40,42,45,48,53,54,56,57,59,60,126
Nimitz, Capt. C. (Jnr.)	47,60
Nishihara, Major	69,74,75,77
OBOE Operations	84,92,93,94,101,102,103,104,114,
	118,125,128,130
Okamoto, Lt.	46
O'Keefe, Capt. E.O.	30,35,36,43
Olsen, Sgt. F.G. later Lieut.	35,36,49,55,56,120
Orr, Pte. J.	98
Osman Panjang	40
Ota, Lt.	46
Otsuka, Colonel	67,79,112,120
Ouyen, Lt.Gen. Van	94
Parsons, Cdr. Charles	13,18,19,20,29,30,61,87
Phillips, Mr.	73
Picone, Capt.	2
Percival, Pte. E.J.	131
PETER Operation	94
POCOMOKE, USN	115
Prentice, Capt.	101
PYTHON Operations	30,34,40,42,43,44,50,54,60,66,67,
	70,75,112,129
Quadra, Cpl.	26
QUEENFISH, USS	90
Rajak, Abdul	123
Ranger, Wing Cdr.	103,104,105
Reither, Pte. H.	11,126
REDFIN, USS	47,48,49
Richards,	71
Richardson, Capt. R.J.	24,25
Ripley, Flt.Lt.	125
Roberts, Colonel (AIB)	43,66
Rodgers, Brigadier (Dir.M.I.)	31
Roffey,	74
Rooney, Group Capt.	111
Rosenquist, Capt. H.A.	88
Rudwick, Lt. A.J.	40,45,46,47,50,69
Russell, Sgt. W.	126

Sampura, P.C.	125
Sayam	78
Saurez, Colonel L.	11,21,26,27,31,38,39,61,62,112,114
Scherger, Air Commodore	86,104,105,118
Sharp, General	16
Short, Pte. N.	11
Simms, Group Capt.	104
Sligo, Lt. N.K.	5
Smith, Lt.Col. Charles S.	13,19,20,61
Smith, Albert Y.	19
Smith, Mr. (G.G. BNB)	71
Sneed, Bessie	95
Spoor, Colonel S.H.	94,100,111
SQUIRREL Operation	101
Steele, Capt. R.	24,25,26,27,28,30,31,32,40,44,86,87
Stefanides, Capt. (USN)	122
Stevens, Sgt. A.	73,74
Sticpewich, W.O.	11,68,126
Suga, Major	5,7,67,68,74,75
Sutherland, Lt.General	23
Sutcliffe, Capt. D.S.	120,123,124,125
Tait, William	18
Takakuwa, Capt.	10,11,42,99,120,126
Takahara, (Guard)	11,126
TAMBOR, USS	13,20
Taylor, Dr.	71
Teruchi, Marshal	96
Thompson, Pte. J.	99
TINOSA, USS	40
Tipping, Pte. N.	131
Tojo, P.M. Japan	129
Toyama (Clerk)	77
Tsuji, Colonel	15
TUNA, USS	122,123
Valera, Lt.	38,39,43,44,50,61
Varley, Brigadier A.	83
VICTOR Operations	91,92,93,114,129
Villamor, Major	19
Wagner, Lt. Charles	24,25,26,27,28,40,44
Wallace, W.O.	5,30,31,32,83
Walsh, Lt.Col.	5,75,83

Watanabe, Haruo Capt.	10
Watanabe, Major Yoshio	120,126
Wainwright, General	14,15,16
Warfe, Lt. Col.	111
Wells, Lt. R.	6,73,74
Wells, Brigadier	125
Wells, Pte. F.	118
Wells, Pte. M.	118
Weis, Capt.	40
Weynton, Lt.	6,71,73
Whimpster, Lt.Col.	24
Whitehead, Brigadier D.A.	102,103,111
Whitehead, Captain	102
Wills, Brigadier K. (AIB)	32,66,106,125
Wong, Mr.	7,68,96
Woods, Lt. L.J.	35,56
Wong Sue, Sgt.	120,124
Wu Kokuang	74
Yamamoto Unit	7
Yamamoto, Capt.	67,96
Yamawaki, Lt.General	75,76,77,78,79
Young, Lt.	27
Young, W.F. TM2C USN	53

NOTES

CHAPTER 1

Captain Hoshijima, the POW Camp Commandant at Sandakan, was charged under the War Crimes Act on four counts of ill-treatment, cruelty and torture, failing to provide adequate food and medical care, and permitting underfed prisoners to be employed on heavy manual work. He was found Guilty on all charges and hanged at Rabaul in 1946.

Hoshijima's defense claimed he received instructions from Higher Authority in regard to rations and administration of prisoners of war.

Colonel Suga, the Commander of all Prisoners of War in Burma, committed suicide while awaiting interrogation.

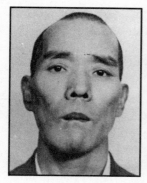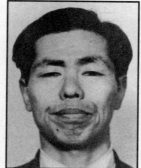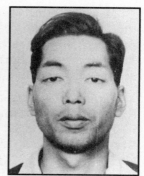

CHAPTER 3

Lt.Col. Egami   Capt. Watanabe Haruo   Capt. Tsutsui
Chief Judge   Prosecutor   Junior Judge

Together with Major Nishihara comprised the Court for the Trial of Capt. Matthews. The same Court tried approximately 30 other Australians for violation of Prisoner of War Regulations. They were later moved to Outram Road Gaol, Singapore, to serve their sentence. Lt. Wells identified Capt. Tsutsui. He stated: "This officer deliberately ignored requests for Defending Counsel and deliberately misinterpreted answers by Capt. Matthews and myself, contradicting questions by the Court. He personally asked the President for the respective verdicts." Wells testified that Capt. Watanabe personally interrogated Capt. Matthews and himself at Kuching and forewarned them of the Court's probable decision. On appealing to him that Capt. Matthews' evidence regarding the so-called riot in Sandakan was deliberately misconstrued by Osawa (Hoshijima's POW Camp Interpreter) he declined to contact Sandakan and said: "Justice would take its course".

Reports stated Major Nishihara died by rifle fire with his gaoler the day before cessation of hostilities.

The fate of Rudwick, McKenzie and Brandis was not disclosed to their respective families until the Author informed them. Previously they had been advised by the Commanding Officer of 'Z' Special Unit in December 1945 they were lost at sea after leaving Sandakan. This information was first collected by Sgt. W.A.C. Russell of S.R.D. in October/November 1945. Relatives were misinformed by a former 'Z' Special operative who had served in Borneo they were executed by the sword. The Army could have informed the relatives in 1946 when their bodies were recovered and identified.

Major Nishihara has been described as a Judge and Prosecutor at the Trials of Captain Matthews, Lt. Rudwick and Sgts. McKenzie and Brandis. Nishihara's real role was Judicial Officer of the 37th Japanese Army in Borneo, he was to ensure the Trial Judges carried out the wishes of the War Ministry.

Yamawaki Masataka, former Lt General, Commander of the 37th Army, Maeda Toshimitsu, Matsumoto Tomeyoshi and Kanazawa Kisou, were charged for the murder of Rudwick, McKenzie and Brandis. The Trial took place in 1950 and they were found Not Guilty.

The Court Authorities advised by direction the information contained in the proceedings will not be disclosed to the Press.

CHAPTER 5

This order of battle for R.A.A.F. Units included in the Tarakan convoy details the comparison of Army-R.A.A.F. personnel and vehicles. When it was found the airfield would not be serviceable for some time some of these Units were allocated elsewhere.

Order of Battle – R.A.A.F. Units

Unit	Pers	Veh	Remarks
76 F Sqn)	311	32	Plus Air Ech 24 pers
77 F Sqn) 81 F Wing,	311	32	Plus Air Ech 24 pers
82 F Sqn)	311	32	Plus Air Ech 24 pers
452 Sqn)	311	32	Plus Air Ech 24 pers
22 Attack Sqn)	348	34	Plus Air Ech 72 pers
30 Attack Sqn)77 Attack Wing	343	34	Plus Air Ech 72 pers
31 Attack Sqn)	348	34	Plus Air Ech 72 pers
Det 16 Air Op Flt	20	3	
Det 113 Air Sea Rescue Flt	64	5	Plus Air Ech 40 pers
Adv Ech 1st Tactical Air Force	240	13	
Det 4 Radio installation			
Maint. Unit	60	6	
Det 10 Replenishing Centre	34	5	
Det 2 Malaria Control Unit	7	2	
Det 11 Postal Unit	7	2	
Det 9 Tpt Mov Office	19	3	
Det Service Police Unit	11	1	
Bomb Disposal Unit	10	1	
Det Defence Pool Unit	130	1	
Det Air Fmn Sigs	80	18	

HQ Task Force	62	3
HQ 77 Attack Wing	57	17
Air Support Sec	50	14
47 Op Base Unit	345	27
26 Repair & Service Unit	432	66
23 Med Clearing Sta	34	8
27 Air Stores Pk	74	30
HQ 84 F Wind 81	59	17
14 Repair & Service Unit	432	66
28 Med Clearing Sta	34	8
29 Air Stores Pk	74	30
114 Mob Fighter Control Unit	285	52
167 Radar Sta	31	4
168 Radar Sta	31	4
308 Radar Sta	31	4
309 Radar Sta	31	4
312 Radar Sta	31	4
354 Radar Sta	31	4
355 Radar Sta	31	4
1st Airfield Constr Sqn	577	176
Det 61 Airfield Constr Wind	15	3
TOTAL RAAF UNITS	5732	835

SUMMARY

	Pers	Veh
Divisional Units	6311	576
2 Aust Beach Group	2096	273
1 Aust Corp Tps allotted	2486	452
1 Aust Base Sub Area	491	81
	11,384	1,382

CHAPTER 8

General Baba inherited the responsibility of the prisoners of war in Borneo when he took command of the 37 Army in January 1945. Up until this time his command had no authority over POW Administration. He was charged for having given the command to move the prisoners from Sandakan to Ranau. He was found guilty of having ordered the marches and was hanged at Rabaul.

He stated at his Appeal: "At the end of January 1945, I proceeded to my new post in Borneo, when a storm caused by the enormous material power, and powerful and skilful leading for operations of the Allied Forces began to rage, and I continued the battles as if I was propping up a big tree about to fall down. As the offensive by the Allied Forces developed and its wind-power increased, various unexpected incidents occurred and the results were as if leaves were blown off, branches were broken and trunks were fallen down. Such conditions continued until the cessation of hostilities. Unfortunately, I could not see the fruits of my efforts. I hereby express my sincere feeling of pity towards the spirits of the many dead persons, their surviving families and people of the Commonwealth of Australia, and at the same time I make an apology to all of them."

BABA Masao